Chambe

terms to

squirm

200 words you shouldn't use

C000173046

Chambers
terms to make you squirm
200 words you shouldn't use

Chambers

CHAMBERS
An imprint of Chambers Harrap Publishers Ltd
7 Hopetoun Crescent, Edinburgh, EH7 4AY

Chambers Harrap is an Hachette UK company

© Chambers Harrap Publishers Ltd, 2009

Chambers® is a registered trademark of Chambers Harrap Publishers Ltd

First published by Chambers Harrap Publishers Ltd 2009

A CIP catalogue record for this book is available from the British Library.

ISBN 978 0550 10475 5

10 9 8 7 6 5 4 3 2 1

We have made every effort to mark as such all words which we believe to
be trademarks.

Text: Elspeth Summers
Publishing Manager: Morven Dooner

www.chambersharrap.co.uk

Designed by Chambers Harrap Publishers Limited
typeset in Arial and Adobe Caslon by Chambers Harrap Publishers Ltd,
Edinburgh
Illustrations by Iain McIntosh
Printed and bound in Great Britain by Clays Ltd, St Ives plc

Terms to Make You Squirm or why you should avoid these 200 words

The breadth of vocabulary available to the English speaker or writer is such that it is easy to panic when faced with the decision: which word should I use? Other books, not least our own *Chambers Address to Impress* (subtitled *200 Words You Should Use*), offer useful advice on the words you should introduce into your lexicon, and the best way to use them in everyday speech.

Terms to Make You Squirm, however, offers the user the reverse: 200 misused, overused, clichéd and confused words from current English, all with real examples from books, magazines, newspapers and websites. The sources of these examples range from broadsheets to tabloids, fiction to non-fiction, highbrow to popular culture. These citations are included not to embarrass or accuse the authors and editors responsible: rather they are intended to illustrate the pitfalls and hazards of the English language and to act as a reminder that no-one is immune.

This book includes words and phrases you should use with care or, in some cases, avoid altogether. A typical entry explains the meaning of the word, words or phrase in question, followed by some examples showing real usage. Entries contain guidance on correct use or suggest replacements for the overused term or clichéd phrase. Some entries contain etymological information that the user may find helpful.

The book is divided into four sections: misused words, overused words, clichés and confusables.

Misused words
The use or misuse of certain English words is always likely to cause lively debate. These include such old favourites as **aggravate, decimate** and **fulsome**. More recent additions to their number are **unique, sat, methodology** and **young**.

Overused words
The huge number of words in the English language (a figure impossible to establish but reckoned in the hundreds of thousands) ought to preclude the overuse of any one in particular but this is not the case. Some of these overused words are long-time offenders: **nice**. However, many of them are relatively new coinages or meanings which offer an intriguing insight into life in the 21st century: **journey, ownership, closure, awesome** and **24/7**.

Clichés
An informal survey of family and friends about their most-hated clichés would doubtless provide a list containing dozens of examples. These are the phrases that provoke a groan each time they are read or (more often) heard, the formulaic space-fillers that punctuate sentences without contributing to their meaning: **at the end of the day, at this moment in time, in a very real sense**, and **tick all the boxes**.

Confusables
English has numerous 'confusables': these are the pairs or groups of words that are often used incorrectly in place of each other. The confusion can arise for several reasons: similar spelling (**continuous and continual**); identical or similar pronunciation (**compliment** and

complement); closely related meaning (**abuse** and **misuse**); or just straightforward misunderstanding (**downfall** and **drawback**).

Terms to Make You Squirm provides easy-to-understand guidance on 200 of the trickiest and commonest usage problems in English and offers a fascinating snapshot of the language as it really is.

aggravate

Aggravate means to make a bad situation worse and many people consider the use of **aggravate** to mean 'irritate or annoy' to be incorrect. It is therefore better to avoid this, especially in written English.

> But I have a great deal of money tied up in this city, and cannot afford to **aggravate** important men without good reason.
>
> SUSANNA GREGORY *A Conspiracy of Violence*

> She wrote: 'Howard has been buying me some jewellery but he calls me 15 or 20 times a day – it drives me crazy. I love him but he **aggravates** me sometimes'.
>
> *Daily Record*

> She said that the prime minister had made the statement out of political motives since what concerned him was keeping his coalition together and not **aggravating** the opposition.
>
> *Jerusalem Post*

> Ganguly's turning out late for the toss had **aggravated** rival skipper Steve Waugh no end, prompting him to mention the incident later in his autobiography as well.
>
> *Times of India*

Instead of **aggravate**, use 'irritate', 'annoy', 'provoke' or 'exasperate'.

amount

You should not use **amount** with a plural count noun; it should be used with uncount nouns.

> 'Smuggled drugs come through from Afghanistan in the east to other parts of Iran and increasing amounts of arms have come from Iraq in the west since the fall of Saddam', he says.
>
> *Financial Times*

The word to use with plural count nouns is 'number' – 'increasing numbers of arms'.

> He spent an extraordinary **amount** of Packer's money, which Kerry didn't mind because Sam got results.
>
> *Sydney Morning Herald*

> Fellow fishermen said they dropped anchor for the night on Jan 25 but fell into a deep sleep, probably helped by large **amounts** of alcohol.
>
> *Daily Telegraph*

> I am ashamed and angry at the **amount** of litter on North Carolina roads and streets. It's disgusting, depressing, and embarrassing.
>
> *The News & Observer*

> The Army is finding that the **amount** of time soldiers enjoy between Iraq tours has been shrinking this year.
>
> *Los Angeles Times*

> A lack of rain will affect mostly those who farm crops such as wheat, soybeans and corn, which require large **amounts** of water.
>
> *G&M National*

anticipate

Many people consider the use of **anticipate** to mean 'expect' to be incorrect. You should therefore avoid this, especially in written English. **Anticipate** means to foretell, or to use, spend or deal with in advance.

'It was supposed to be finished inside a year, but there was a great deal more work involved in it than I had **anticipated**'.
Belfast Telegraph

The band will bring their *Just Doin' It* tour to Live at Scone Palace on Sunday, July 29. It is **anticipated** the band will play to a 15,000 crowd.

Daily Record

Forensic examinations are ongoing at the address where the body remains. It is **anticipated** that a post mortem will be carried out later this afternoon.

News Wales

I followed the receptionist obediently into the room where Dr Glassman was waiting. He was much younger than I had **anticipated**.

SUSAN HOWATCH *The Rich are Different*

This month the monetary policy committee voted to keep rates unchanged, but an increase is widely **anticipated** in November.
The Guardian

Alternatives to **anticipate** include 'foresee', 'expect', 'predict' and 'envisage'.

auspicious

The adjective **auspicious** is derived from the noun **auspice**, which is from Latin *avis*, meaning 'a bird' and *specere*, meaning 'to observe': an **auspice** is an omen drawn from observing birds, especially a good omen. Therefore, something **auspicious** is favourable or has good omens for success. Literally, an **auspicious** occasion is one that looks as if it will bring good fortune; however, many people misunderstand this use and assume that an auspicious occasion is one that is special or joyful. An occasion may be auspicious *and* special, but these are two different things.

> Is Swansea's Chris Coleman a better coach than Govan Godfather Alex Ferguson? On this **auspicious** day for Fulham, you might be tempted to say so.
>
> *Daily Telegraph*

> 'I have been proud to be in office as this year's president, representing passionate, inspiring and gutsy individuals, in a place as **auspicious** as Aberystwyth'.
>
> *The Guardian*

> So the Newcomer Tour got rolling before the lunch hour did. On a Tuesday. In the rain. Not the most **auspicious** time to catch the vibe of the city's dining scene.
>
> *Philadelphia Online*

Take care when using **auspicious**: if you don't mean 'showing signs of good fortune to come', don't use it.

consensus

A **consensus** is an agreement in opinion. There is no need to add 'of opinion' to **consensus** because it is already contained within the meaning of **consensus**.

> It was the general **consensus** of opinion that if the little Mezentine had had to install the things himself, he'd have given a bit more thought to stuff like that.
>
> PD JAMES *Devices and Desires*

> **Consensus** of opinion in Liverpool seemed to be that the passing of a blanket ban on smoking in pubs by a huge Commons majority was merely a nod to the inevitable.
>
> *Liverpool News*

> While that must be open to question, the **consensus** of opinion is that the ante-post favourite is well drawn in stall 15.
>
> *The Guardian*

> The **consensus** of opinion was that it had no chance of being accepted as a whole, and that cherry-picking certain issues, such as wider council representation and compliance changes, was more acceptable.
>
> *Daily Mail*

> 'This is also propelled by the **consensus** of opinion amongst scientists about the value of olive oil as part of a balanced eating plan'.
>
> *BBC Magazine*

Alternatives to **consensus** include 'agreement', 'unanimity' and 'concord'.

decimate

The verb **decimate** is a controversial one. Its original meaning is 'to take or destroy the tenth part of' or 'to punish by killing every tenth man'. It is derived from Latin *decimus*, meaning 'tenth'. Another sense, 'to reduce very heavily', has developed from this original meaning, but many people consider this to be incorrect, even though it has been in existence since the 17th century. When using **decimate** in this sense the object ought to be the whole of a group or number, not a part of it.

> And unlike many other islands in the archipelago Asian logging companies have not yet **decimated** the forests.
>
> *Sydney Morning Herald*

> 'This time last year England were **decimated** by injuries and did not have replacements who could turn a game but they showed in the last 20 minutes on Saturday what a good team they will turn out to be'.
>
> *The Guardian*

> The Environment Agency will be putting almost one million roach, dace, chub, bream and barbel into neglected waters after fish-guzzling cormorants and pollution **decimated** stocks.
>
> *The Sun*

> H5N1, which has **decimated** poultry stocks in southeast Asia and caused the death of 62 people, is now knocking on Europe's door after spreading from Asia into Siberia.
>
> *The Herald*

Although this sense of **decimate** is long established, be aware that some people may object to its use.

dichotomy

A **dichotomy** is a division into two strongly contrasted groups or opinions. Another sense has developed from this: a problem or situation in which there is a clear split or difference of opinion. This meaning of **dichotomy** is generally considered to be incorrect.

> Outside in the garden there is the peculiarly, oddly infuriating English **dichotomy** of rain and a hosepipe ban.
>
> *The Times*

> There should not be a **dichotomy** between education and training; the economy needs both and they are not incompatible.
>
> *The Guardian*

> 'There's also a delicious **dichotomy** at work, a juxtaposition of demure lady (the dresses are modestly tailored; no plunging necklines here) and wild child'.
>
> *New York Post*

> And it points up the jarring **dichotomy** of the festival world. On the surface, it's about gentility and art. But with at least 600 fests vying for attention, there's fierce competition for money and prestige.
>
> *Variety*

Alternatives for this sense of **dichotomy** include 'contradiction', 'inconsistency' and 'incongruity'.

dilemma

In strict usage a **dilemma** is a choice between two eminently undesirable alternatives. It has come to mean 'any predicament or problem', but some people object to this usage.

Do you have a menu **dilemma** for Bill Granger?
Sydney Morning Herald

It needed further thought. For now his immediate problem was what to wear for dinner tonight – every woman's **dilemma**. Wyl scowled, hating that he should be concerned with such things.
Fiona McIntosh *Blood and Memory*

Having a baby will cost me hundreds of thousands over my lifetime, according to one report. Parenthood is seen as a mum's **dilemma**.
The Guardian

Angelina said their biggest **dilemma** was exactly what country their next child should be from. She added: 'We want to find another brother or sister in the world for our family'.
Daily Record

The **dilemma** for researchers is to figure out how to protect neurons from the lethal doses of calcium without causing more damage to learning and memory.
Science Daily

Alternatives for this sense of **dilemma** include 'problem', 'predicament', 'difficulty', 'quandary' and 'plight'.

disinterested

In the 17th century **disinterested** had two meanings:
'not interested' and 'not influenced by private feelings
or considerations'. The first of these meanings became
obsolete but the second remained. In the 20th century
the first meaning made a reappearance but many people
objected to its use, preferring to keep the distinction
between **uninterested** for 'not interested' and **disinterested**
for 'impartial'. Over the years, this distinction has been
gradually eroded, but some people still maintain that
disinterested does not mean 'not interested'.

> She always looked elegant, despite the fact that she claimed to
> be **disinterested** in fashion.
>
> *Sydney Morning Herald*

> 'I was disillusioned, though, with the police. They were totally
> **disinterested** and did not investigate the crime in any way'.
>
> *Daily Telegraph*

> Mr Blair insisted people did not feel **disinterested** with
> politics but disempowered.
>
> *The Herald*

> Children who lack independent mobility from an early age
> sometimes develop 'learned helplessness', where they become
> **disinterested** and withdrawn.
>
> *Daily Mail*

> With this year's turning back of the clock, the 14.5 million
> Americans susceptible to Seasonal Affective Disorder may
> begin feeling fatigued, worthless, **disinterested**, even suicidal.
>
> *Science Daily*

You can make a plausible argument for either view.

enormity

Many people object to the use of **enormity** to mean 'immenseness or vastness' in any context. Others consider it acceptable to use **enormity** when talking of the large scale of something non-physical, such as a task, a problem or an achievement. Most people consider it unacceptable to use **enormity** for physical things, such as buildings, countries or bodies. In those contexts, **enormousness** is preferred.

While Theron acknowledged the **enormity** of the task awaiting his team, he said they would give the Sharks a good run for their money.

Rugby World

But I want our fans and players to understand the **enormity** of our achievement in getting to the final. What we've done on limited money is unbelievable.

Daily Record

Pain etched on her face, grief reflected in the tears she cried, the distraught mother sobbed 'my baby, my baby' as she collapsed on her murdered son's coffin, overwhelmed by the **enormity** of her grief.

Belfast Telegraph

'If you focus on the **enormity** of the problem, you'll never get started', says Kline, who has cared for hundreds of HIV-positive children over the years.

Newsweek

Although he was moved by the **enormity** of the sacrifice Livia had made, another part of him was appalled that she had been able to do it at all.

ANTHONY CAPELLA *The Wedding Officer*

fascination

The noun **fascination** is one that must be used carefully. If you say 'Eve has a fascination for George', who is fascinated? Eve or George? Strictly, in this sentence, it is Eve who is fascinating and George who is fascinated by her: this is possibly the opposite of what is intended by the statement.

> 'But my father was with the Pune police and, hence, right from my childhood, I had a **fascination** for the police force and defence services', he said.
>
> *Times of India*

> But Péladan certainly had a **fascination** for Leonardo, devoting two scholarly books to him, besides being the first to translate Leonardo's notebooks and manuscripts in the Institut de France into French.
>
> LYNN PICKNETT *The Sion Revelation*

The person or object that 'has the fascination' is the fascinating one, and you should bear this in mind when you use **have a fascination for**.

> 'I can understand that – aeroplanes have always had a **fascination for** me, too'.
>
> MARJORIE ECCLES *The Gil Mayo Mysteries*

You can also avoid this ambiguity by using 'have a fascination with' or 'hold a fascination for'.

> When he was a kid he **had a fascination with** baseball umpires.
>
> *The Guardian*

> And there was no doubt that Violette **held a fascination for** Vera.
>
> SARAH HELM *A Life in Secrets*

feasible

Something **feasible** is able to be done or achieved. **Feasible** comes from French *faisable*, meaning 'that can be done', from the verb *faire*, meaning 'to do'. There is another sense of **feasible** that means 'probable or likely'. Some people consider this usage to be incorrect.

> The authors suggest that it is **feasible** that certain chemicals could be a factor in causing cancer but do not find compelling scientific evidence to prove a link.
> *The Guardian*

> It does not seem **feasible** that David Dein, the Arsenal vice-chairman, would accept such a humiliating loss, no matter what the footballing merits of the proposed transfer.
> *The Times*

> 'It was not **feasible** Caroline took her own life', Mr Byrne said at the time. 'She was thrown off that cliff'.
> *Sydney Morning Herald*

> As scientists currently think that our planet's abundance of water, essential for life, arrived by interstellar snowball, then it is **feasible** that other planets have been equally lucky and given rise to a species capable of galactic travel.
> *The Herald*

> It is **feasible** that we will have further rain in Japan or Brazil, or both.
> *The Times*

Alternatives for this sense of **feasible** include 'probable', 'possible' and 'likely'.

fortuitous

A **fortuitous** meeting is one that happens by chance.
Fortuitous is sometimes used to mean 'fortunate or lucky',
but some people object to this usage. It is therefore better to
avoid using it in formal, especially written, contexts.

> The Cowboys appeared to me as though they now don't expect
> anything good to happen for them. I have always seen them
> as something of a **fortuitous** team who played for more than
> their fair share of luck.
>
> *Sydney Morning Herald*

> Still, the current oil price drop has triggered warning bells
> about the course of Mexico's future fiscal revenue and
> spending. This is politically **fortuitous** for the government.
>
> *The Economist*

> Charlton were deservedly in front after 27 minutes, even if
> their goal was slightly **fortuitous**.
>
> *Daily Telegraph*

> England were **fortuitous** not to lose Paul Collingwood as
> three times in his first half-a-dozen runs he might have been
> run out.
>
> *Daily Mail*

> The upbeat assessment of market prospects indicates that
> Matheson is likely to have taken the reins of the company at a
> **fortuitous** time.
>
> *The Herald*

You can use 'lucky', 'fortunate' and 'timely' as alternatives to
this meaning of **fortuitous**.

fulsome

The original meaning of **fulsome** is 'nauseatingly obsequious or complimentary'. It has also come to mean 'lavish or abundant', but without the negative connotation of the original meaning. Therefore 'fulsome praise' can either be praise that is so excessive as to make the hearer want to vomit, or it can be praise that is generous and unstinting without making the hearer feel sick. In writing the reader has to rely on the context to know which is meant. For that reason, it is best to avoid **fulsome** in the second sense, as the meaning is so often ambiguous. It is possibly to read either meaning into **fulsome** in the following citations.

> And by a grim and curious coincidence it turns out she's Venetian herself, or so it suits the entrepreneur to style her in his **fulsome** biography of the actress.
>
> MICHELLE LOVRIC *The Remedy*

> But almost as soon as his **fulsome** tributes to the 'Land of Smiles' appeared, brickbats and allegations from readers followed, some apparently from disgruntled Britons, and focused on the country's seedier side.
>
> *Daily Telegraph*

> So well that Freddy Shepherd yesterday declared he would not swap his manager for Sir Alex Ferguson. After such **fulsome** praise from the chairman, sceptics might have anticipated a home defeat.
>
> *Daily Telegraph*

Alternatives to **fulsome** include 'generous', 'lavish' and 'abundant'.

join

When used transitively, **join** means 'to bring together', as in 'join these two pieces of wood'. The definition of **join** contains the idea of 'bringing together' so it is unnecessary to add 'together' when **join** is taking a direct object.

'Either the government has got to **join departments together** and get these changes made, or we've going to have to ask the European Commission to take Britain to court and make sure that we're protecting our environment properly'.

BBC News

By analogy with an electronic chip full of transistors, the most basic requirement is to **join the bits together** with wires.

Science Daily

The questions have also been reasonably asked in the past when trade buyers have been involved in takeovers. The difference is that there are strategic reasons a trade buyer can make money by **joining similar businesses together**.

Sydney Morning Herald

He **joined his hands together** in a gesture that seemed close to hand-wringing.

ALEXANDER McCALL SMITH *The Right Attitude to Rain*

The nanotubes are transferred to metal surfaces that are coated with solder – a metal alloy that is melted to **join metallic surfaces together**.

Science Daily

No meaning would be lost by removing **together** from the above examples.

large-size *and* small-size

The adjective **large** is defined as 'great in size', and **small** is defined as 'little in size'. It is therefore unnecessary to add 'size' or 'sized' to these adjectives as this information is redundant.

Or, better still, she'd like to take one of her **large-size** cappuccino mugs, fill it up to the brim with frothy milk and pour the whole lot over his head.

DEBORAH WRIGHT *Love Eternally*

Domestic output of **large-sized** LCD screens grew almost 250 per cent last year, according to DisplayBank.

Computing UK

'Depending on when and where you look back in time, native peoples were either living in harmony with nature or eating their way through a vast array of **large-sized**, attractive prey species'.

Science Daily

'She's been driving a Ford Explorer since 1998', said Jay Kravitz, eyeing the new **small-size** Volvo for his wife.

Philadelphia Online

Pasta: Don't cut the strands with your knife, and avoid that business of using the bowl of a spoon to twirl. If it's **small-size** pasta – ziti, penne and the like – use only a fork.

Seattle Times

Around 700 **small-sized** companies across the country took part the survey.

RTE News Online

Do not add 'size' or 'sized' to adjectives of scale: the adjective alone is enough.

majority

Some people think you should use **majority** with count nouns only, and for uncount nouns you should use 'most of'. However, it is not unusual to find **majority** being used with uncount nouns.

> The other significant change for publishers involves contextual truth, a defence which excuses those who get the great **majority** of the story right.
>
> *Sydney Morning Herald*

> The **majority** of spam is sent through zombie computers, which are vast networks of hijacked personal computers infected by rogue software, which is used to send bulk e-mail messages.
>
> *G&M National*

> Most studies suggest that of the 500 or so bacterial species in the mouth, Streptococcus mutans causes the **majority** of decay.
>
> *Science Daily*

> 'I will shake the manager's hand. The **majority** of the time we got on fine, and it was only in recent weeks that we didn't communicate as well as maybe we should have'.
>
> *The Sun*

> 'For the vast **majority** of our marriage, the last 20 of our 28-year marriage, my husband and I lived among the most lavish of American lifestyles', Janet Burkle stated in a September 2003 divorce filing.
>
> *Seattle Times*

To satisfy the purists, you should use **'most'** in the above examples.

masterful

In strict usage, the correct meaning of **masterful** is 'showing great authority or power'. People often use **masterful** when they mean 'masterly', which means 'showing great skill', but this is considered by many to be wrong.

> 'With Lionsgate, we have a terrific partner who shares our conviction that Larry Brown's **masterful** novel will make for a great movie'.
>
> *Empire*

> He was barely on the job when he came to hate her and everything she had accomplished, and he became **masterful** at showing his contempt in small ways, by neglecting whatever had been associated with Scarpetta.
>
> PATRICIA CORNWELL *Trace*

> The author is **masterful** at portraying the emotional complexities of family and community through the eyes of a precocious youngster.
>
> *Seattle Times*

> By no means all bloggers are Pepys – Pepys never blathers on, as bloggers are prone to do – but Pepys would have been a **masterful** blogger.
>
> *The Times*

> The journalist, Alan Zarembo, did a **masterful** job of describing one man's quest to save his own life.
>
> *Newsweek*

> Dylan is not only a **masterful** songwriter, he's also one of the best pop singers of all time.
>
> *The Slate*

It is best if you observe the distinction between **masterful**, meaning 'powerful' and **masterly**, meaning 'skilful'.

methodology

Methodology is the system of methods and rules applicable to research or work in a given science or art. It is not a synonym for 'method'.

'Part of my **methodology** in assessing a problem is to consider every option no matter how outlandish'.

Yachting & Boating World

Although not everyone will agree with Greenpeace's **methodology**, its ranking still has some merit.

The Economist

His **methodology** for stock selection is to conduct significant research not only into the sector in which a company operates but also the capabilities and track record of its management team.

The Herald

They've applied the same **methodology** to their last four albums, and as contrarian or pretentious as it sounds, it's working.

Newsweek

It is an old **methodology** of the Indian government to divert the attention of Indians from the chronic problems of poverty and disease by externalizing the issue.

Christian Science Monitor

'The nature of the accused's **methodology** is to target vulnerable complainants, build trust with them, make them dependent on him for drugs and money and then to abuse that trust'.

Sydney Morning Herald

In the above examples **methodology** could be replaced with 'method', 'process' or 'procedure'.

occur *and* happen

When an event **occurs** or **happens**, it takes place, but not by arrangement. Something that you do not expect **occurs** or **happens**; something you have planned **takes place**.

> The Vienna meetings **occurred** as the UN nears discussions about possible sanctions on Iran for its defiance of an August 31 deadline for stopping production of nuclear fuel.
>
> *Sydney Morning Herald*

> This dinner **occurred** in February 2004 while Mr Rana – later Lord Rana – was still at the centre of an investigation by the DoE over the flattening of his listed Tillie and Henderson factory building in Derry.
>
> *Belfast Telegraph*

> The warrant also said Daniel Flannery, a team captain and resident of the house where the party **occurred**, admitted hiring the dancers under a false name.
>
> *Time*

> The christening **occurred** only two weeks after Lady Jane Grey and her husband Guildford Dudley had been tried and found guilty of high treason.
>
> MARY S LOVELL *Bess of Hardwick*

> 'People feel like they're on top of the world, then the wedding **happens** and they don't feel so hot anymore', she says.
>
> *Newsweek*

Use 'take place' for planned events and keep **occur** and **happen** for the unexpected.

over-simplistic

The definition of **simplistic** is 'tending to oversimplify'. It is therefore unnecessary to precede it with 'over-', as the idea of 'over-' or 'excessively' is already contained within **simplistic**.

Simon Hughes, the party's chair and a London MP, said: 'The prime minister is just plain wrong and **over-simplistic** about gun and knife crime'.

The Guardian

James Lewis, a US foreign-policy analyst at CSIS, called Bush's assertion **over-simplistic**. 'There's a grain of truth in Bush saying it's better to fight them there rather than here, but it's also overstated'.

Seattle Times

CNW's methodology may not be perfect – it is disputed by Toyota – but it beats our Government's horribly **over-simplistic** 'Green Rating', which makes some tax discs costlier than others.

Daily Telegraph

Conscious, perhaps, that this could sound a little **over-simplistic**, Craig adds: 'It is not about being a Pollyanna, or about shifting from one extreme to another overnight'.

The Herald

Mr Muttalibi said the view that you cannot talk to terrorists is very **over-simplistic**.

BBC News

Mr Reid states: 'Mr Cameron's analysis is **over-simplistic** and sadly one-sided'.

Daily Telegraph

preferable

A **preferable** option or object is more desirable than another option or object. The definition of **preferable** contains the idea of 'more', so it is incorrect to put 'more' in front of it. **Preferable** should be followed by 'to', not 'than'.

Friends of the Earth says that, purely in terms of reducing greenhouse-gas emissions, buying a more fuel-efficient new car is broadly speaking more **preferable** than choosing a less fuel-efficient second-hand car.

The Guardian

If you think cycling around the traffic-congested streets of a busy city like New York is only slightly more **preferable** to wrestling an alligator, you're wrong.

Daily Mirror

Any of those events would have been infinitely more **preferable** to watching the dross 42,192 fans paid good money to endure on Saturday.

The Sun

'An independent commission would be much more **preferable** to a takeover by a federal government'.

Sydney Morning Herald

In matters of mercy, Martemus said, a known enemy was always more **preferable** than an unknown.

R Scott Bakker *The Warrior-Prophet*

'But a mortgage is far more preferable to having any consumer debt, such as credit cards, auto loans, etc', says Mr Huller.

Christian Science Monitor

prodigal

A **prodigal** person is wasteful and extravagant with money. There is a misapprehension that the adjective **prodigal** means 'being welcomed back after an absence'. This has arisen from the biblical story (Luke 15:11-32). This is the parable known as *The Prodigal Son*, in which a young man leaves his father's house, spends all his inheritance on riotous living, falls on hard times, returns to throw himself on his father's mercy, and is welcomed back with feasting and celebration, much to the resentment of his elder brother. The misunderstanding of the meaning of **prodigal** arises when people assume the adjective refers to his welcome after a long absence, rather than to his squandering of money that preceded it.

> But Rooney is back in his pomp and there was also something of the old, title-winning flair and stubbornness about United, and not just because Solskjaer, after a three-year absence, has slipped back into the fold like a **prodigal** son.
>
> *Daily Telegraph*

> *The Godfather*: What's It About? The original and best gangster epic shows the lives of a New York Sicilian Mafia family, as a **prodigal** son returns to take over his father's criminal empire.
>
> *Daily Record*

proximity

Proximity is immediate nearness or closeness in place or time. The idea of 'closeness' is therefore contained within the meaning of the word, so you do not need to precede it with 'close'.

> The **close proximity** of both countries to Iran makes Tbilisi and Baku desirable partners in a potential alliance against Iran.
> *Jerusalem Post*

> In Africa, conditions are ripe for such a disastrous event, as millions of humans live in **close proximity** to birds and health services are poor and overstretched.
> *Daily Telegraph*

> It was generally too hot to cook, and she had quickly come to realise that she didn't like being in such **close proximity** to the servants.
> Marilyn Heward *Mills Cloth Girl*

> Elgar's Falstaff and Holst's At the Boar's Head inhabit different territory from Verdi. Both were written in **close proximity** to the first world war, and each takes Henry IV as its sole source.
> *The Guardian*

> The apparent similarities between the Bailey and Nickel Mines shootings – and their **close proximity** in time – raise experts' concerns about 'copycat' attacks.
> *Christian Science Monitor*

Close proximity may be frequently used, but you should avoid it and use **proximity** instead.

rarely

Rarely means 'seldom, hardly ever'. The meaning contains the idea of 'ever', and so it is unnecessary to add 'ever' after **rarely**.

Romanov was put on the ropes when one shareholder asked why he was **rarely** ever in Scotland.

Daily Record

All the improvements will be paid for out of Home Office funds despite the fact that the Duchess **rarely** ever visits the home she bought after her divorce in 1995.

The Sun

Wolves **rarely** ever attack humans, despite what we have been taught in fairy tales and folklore.

Seattle Times

The man never recognizes anyone for a job well done, yet he never yells at anyone for screwing up. He **rarely** ever cracks a smile or laughs, but he doesn't yell. It's almost like he's a robot.

Time

But we **rarely** ever negotiate the questions we are going to ask. If people say 'I will come on the show but won't talk about this', we tell them to come back when they are ready to talk.

Sydney Morning Herald

Did you have a guidance teacher when you were at school? If you're of my generation, then the chances are that you **rarely** ever saw them.

The Herald

require

Be careful when using **require**. It can take a direct object, as in 'Do you require assistance?' and 'Nuclear energy requires a massive investment'. When used in the passive, it can be followed by an infinitive, as in 'A licensed financial adviser is required to deal with your complaint' and 'Mr Gilbertson would be required to pass on all information'. However, you should avoid the construction **require to**, as many people consider it to be incorrect.

But we are an organisation which **requires** to select people on merit.

Times of India

Rangers supporters, meanwhile, will **require** to cope without bidding farewell to the Frenchman.

The Herald

Thomson may have the advantage of sailing higher speeds even if he **requires** to sail a longer distance.

Yachting & Boating World

That is why I **require** to undertake my afternoon meditation ritual, to prepare myself.

ASHOK BANKER *King of Ayodhya*

Their colleagues will **require** to follow their lead against an Armagh side that, while fielding one of the youngest half-back lines in the country, still retains a hard, seasoned edge.

Belfast Telegraph

'They **required** to see the Egyptian treasures once again. I told them that these things were unfortunately no longer open to the public'.

BARBARA EWING *Rosetta*

safe haven

A **haven** is a place of protection, peace or asylum. It is therefore unnecessary to precede **haven** with 'safe', as the idea of safety is already contained within the word **haven** itself. Nevertheless, the phrase **safe haven** is one that is often heard.

> The widow of the murdered former Russian agent Alexander Litvinenko told last night how her husband thought he had found a **safe haven** in Britain, and said the Russian authorities could be to blame for his death.
>
> *Daily Telegraph*

> Motion pictures have long been a **safe haven** for men of few words, most particularly westerns.
>
> *The Guardian*

> The US has neither confirmed nor denied the reports but says it will stop Somalia becoming a **safe haven** for terrorists.
>
> *BBC News*

> Embroiled in a war for independence between 1991 and 1995, Croatia and its stunning Adriatic coast have only recently become **safe havens** for investors like Schmidt.
>
> *Newsweek*

> They provide employment in rural areas, **safe havens** for wildlife and plenty of great places to go walking, biking or sightseeing.
>
> *The Herald*

> Perception counts – and the perception of schools as **safe havens** is eroding with each new incident.
>
> *Time*

sat

In English, the past continuous tense is formed by the verb 'to be' and the present participle, as in 'I was walking down the street when I saw him'. The present participle of 'sit' is 'sitting', therefore the past continuous is 'He was sitting at the rear of the carriage when the train crashed'. However, it has become common in English for people to form the past continuous tense of 'sit' with **sat**, which is the past tense and past participle of the verb.

> 'I watched through the window and I could see the student was with them as they pulled his room apart. He was **sat** on his bed looking shocked – like a scared rabbit in headlights'.
> *Daily Mirror*

> 'I was about nine or 10 years old. We were **sat** by the ring when it was all happening and I thought: "This is mad. Is this going to happen when I get in?"'
> *The Guardian*

> 'Clyde could see this because I was **sat** at the back of the coach on my own, and he just came up and sat down next to me – just to have a chat'.
> *Sydney Morning Herald*

'I was sat' and its variants are certainly common in spoken English, but they are grammatically incorrect and many people object strongly to their use. They should be avoided, especially in written English.

scarify

To **scarify** is to scratch, cut or break up the surface of something. It is sometimes used jocularly to mean 'scare', but this is non-standard and considered by many people to be unacceptable.

The NYT Company says the job cuts and offshoring of some work are necessary for the financial health of the paper. The union isn't convinced, and in fact, it issued the **scarifying** 'loss of privacy' warning to subscribers.

Times of India

The band, though, don't pause for breath, saving the best until last with the relentless and **scarifying** Blindness. This is a more textured Fall than ever before, and Smith himself looks, for him at least, healthy, hearty and, yes, happy.

The Herald

That photo couldn't be stranger, considering that Ellison's truly **scarifying** film provides *Nightmare USA* with the fire on its front cover.

San Francisco Bay Guardian Online

Here's one **scarifying** film portrayal of a poet that challenges any of us who may be tempted to believe that making poetry tends to improve the character: Johnny Depp as the Earl of Rochester in *The Libertine*.

www.indy.com

It is best to maintain the distinction between **scarify** and scare, unless it is clear you are being jocular.

to be fair

The phrase **to be fair** is inserted into speech or writing when you are making a criticism of someone or something, but you want to acknowledge that there may be a good reason why the person or thing was below the standard expected: for example, 'He played badly but, to be fair, he has only just recovered from a broken leg'. However, people often use **to be fair** when they ought to use 'to be honest'.

'I knew I was coming to Milan as second keeper, but **to be fair** I would have liked to have played more matches', he says.
Sydney Morning Herald

This morning, at a small hotel near Rennes, I'm bashing my brains against the laptop when my mobile buzzes with an interview request from a radio station. The timing, **to be fair,** isn't great, but they keep telling me the big bucks are in broadcasting, so I decide to oblige.
The Times

I went, but I went out into the October dark even more certain that I knew absolutely nothing about men. Alright, **to be fair,** that I knew absolutely nothing about the men in my life.
LAURELL K HAMILTON *Incubus Dreams*

These two phrases do not mean the same, so take care not to confuse them.

transpire

If something **transpires**, it becomes known or comes to light, as in 'It later transpired that Professor Brennan had died in a car crash'. **Transpire** is often used as a synonym for 'happen' or 'occur', although some people object to this.

> Given what had just **transpired** between us, given that her intent was so obvious, I'm embarrassed to admit that I was distracted by her nakedness.
>
> STEPHEN WHITE *Kill Me*

> The film, which is based on events that **transpired** after the massacre of Israeli athletes at the Munich Olympics, has earned $25.2m (£14.26m) after three weekends on limited release.
>
> *BBC Entertainment*

> 'The US Patent and Trademark Office has been somewhat embarrassed by how this thing **transpired**'.
>
> *Computing UK*

> The show begins when the captives are released and strikes just the right balance between the intrigue of what actually **transpired** during the 2-½-day standoff, and the intense bonds that form between friends, lovers, and strangers who survive a crisis together.
>
> *Christian Science Monitor*

Alternatives to this sense of **transpire** include 'happen', 'occur' and 'take place'.

underestimate

To **underestimate** is to estimate or value too low. People often get confused when using **underestimate**. If you say that it is **hard to underestimate** something, this means that the thing is small, insignificant or trivial. In most cases, this is the opposite of what was intended.

> More than 6000 people sit in an enormous tent for graduation day. It is hard to **underestimate** the importance that middle-class Americans put on a college education.
>
> *Sydney Morning Herald*

> As exhibitions of raw courage go, it is hard to **underestimate** the actions of those two probationers, mothers and wives, decent as the day is long, running head tilt into a murderous group of criminals.
>
> *The Herald*

> But that doesn't lessen what's at stake. Civic leaders said it's hard to **underestimate** the importance of Progress Energy, particularly as a catalyst in the renaissance of downtown Raleigh.
>
> *The News & Observer*

> 'It's impossible to **underestimate** the value of that social capital, 'Mr Dodge said. 'It's part of trust, which is easily destroyed, and takes a long time to rebuild'.
>
> *G&M National*

> It is hard to **underestimate** how drastic a cultural change the move is for the youngest of the armed services.
>
> *Los Angeles Times*

If you want to express the importance or size of something, the expression is **hard to overestimate**.

unique

In strict usage **unique** means 'sole' or 'without equal', and it is therefore incorrect to modify it with 'rather' or 'very'. However, in recent years **unique** has developed the sense of 'unusual or special'. This use is very common, but many people still object to it.

'This is a very **unique** ecosystem that is completely isolated from the surface', said Dr Frumkin, a cave researcher in the geography department of Hebrew University in Jerusalem.
G&M National

No matter where you are in the world, Christmas has a very **unique** place in people's affections. And while it may become more commercialised every year, it's the old traditions that continue to make it special.
Daily Record

'Still, for someone with your rather **unique** profile, I'm sure we'll be able to find you something that'll keep you out of mischief'.
Tom Holt *Barking*

'Prince Charles's rather **unique** experience is illustrative of a more general point: performing Shakespeare can be a very emotional experience'.
The Herald

Given that many people object to this use of **unique**, it is better to use alternatives such as 'special', 'unusual', 'extraordinary' or 'exceptional'.

young

When used in combination with a number, the adjective **old** indicates a specified age, as in 'I will soon be 43 years old'. Some people, uncomfortable with the other connotations of **old** (advanced in years, old-fashioned, worn-out, decrepit), have taken to changing the **old** in this combination to **young**. This is especially the case when used in relation to people of advancing years. In this context, **young** is used as an indication of their liveliness, sprightliness and vitality.

> Last year's inaugural Ladies Day Trophy was awarded to Betty Moore who, at 88 years **young**, was its first recipient.
>
> *Yachting & Boating World*

> Janice Marie Farris-Sansing has a birthday on March 25, 2007. She will be 56 **years young** and will be honoured with a party being planned by her grand-daughters, Opal and Elizabeth Alexandra.
>
> *The Sun*

> 'I am going to stick with this case and try this case', Sprague said. 'I am 81 years **young**'.
>
> *Philadelphia Online*

> TV Guide channel pre-show host Joan Rivers is 72 years **young**.
>
> *New York Post*

> A milestone birthday for someone who's 90 years **young** cannot go without speeches.
>
> *Jerusalem Post*

This usage ought to be avoided: it makes no sense and could be seen as patronizing.

110%

Some speakers find that, when describing their commitment to a task, 100% is just not enough. They are doing everything they can – and then some more. From this over-exertion we have the phenomenon of **110%**, **115%** and sometimes even **120%** effort. It may be illogical but it is certainly popular.

A small band of fans has called for a boycott of Casino Royale because they do not agree with the casting of Craig. 'I've been trying to give **110%** from the beginning and maybe after that (the criticism), I was trying to give 115%', said Craig.

BBC Entertainment

'And I know that when he wants something he's **110%** committed and I'll know he'll run through a brick wall'.

The Guardian

'I am not keen to have any imported meats but if we are to have them, let's have them in a form which is **110%** safe'.

Daily Mail

On his performance on the new Manowar album *Gods of War*: 'I put **110%** into each and every track. I have to do that'.

www.metalhammer.co.uk

Last month at the team's post-season banquet, Francis, who often guarded the opponent's best player despite being significantly shorter, was given the John Rudometkin Award as the player who always gave **110%** effort.

Los Angeles Times

'Whatever happens happens. I will go about my business professionally, **120%** committed'.

The Guardian

9/11

9/11 has developed some extended meanings. One is a
terrorist attack resulting in significant loss of life. Another
is the murder of a number of people in one incident, but
not carried out by terrorists. It has also come to mean any
unexpected and important event with serious and long-
lasting consequences. These senses are connected by the idea
of something shocking happening without warning, and the
powerful effect it has on a large number of people.

Amish neighbors and friends are coping with the slayings by
looking inward, relying on themselves and their faith, just as
they have for centuries, to get them through what one Amish
bishop called 'our **9/11**'.

Washington Times

Supporters of the king have rallied to condemn 'Jordan's **9/11**'
which has been claimed by the Al-Qaeda in Iraq group.

BBC News

An independent investigation published this week will heap
fuel on the flames of public doubt by challenging key points in
the official version of what happened during the three violent
September days that are often referred to as 'Russia's **9/11**'.

Christian Science Monitor

In Spain, a day of remembrance on the second anniversary of
what is considered that country's **9/11**.

CNN

'Enron was the **9/11** of the financial markets', says Buell, now
a visiting law professor at the University of Texas, 'but nobody
wanted to be a witness'.

Time

24/7

If a service is available **24/7** or **twenty-four-seven** it is available twenty-four hours a day and seven days a week, that is all the time. This informal phrase originated in America. It is used as an adverb and an adjective.

The new satellite station will run **24/7**, broadcasting 12 hours a day from Al Jazeera's home base in Doha, Qatar, with another four hours each from Washington DC, London and Kuala Lumpur.

Jerusalem Post

For parents who work, arranging childcare over the holidays is difficult, but even those who are able to be home can feel the strain of having their youngsters with them **24/7**.

Daily Record

Toyota operates **24/7** car production plants that make 'just-in-time' requests to suppliers for vehicle parts and other materials via electronic communications.

Computing UK

Electroimpact opened a facility in Wales in 2002 to provide a **24/7** engineering support and maintenance service for the systems installed at Broughton.

News Wales

Chris absolutely loved it when he did Celebrity Big Brother. He said that having the cameras on him **24/7** was one of the highlights of his life.

The Sun

Some alternatives to **24/7** are 'constant' and 'constantly', 'non-stop' and 'round-the-clock'.

absolutely

The adverb **absolutely** is often used as expression of affirmation or agreement in spoken English.

'Is it urgent to find new players? **Absolutely**'. The question is how to find them. Should the Socceroos be used as a development squad, or should we find another way to do it?
Sydney Morning Herald

'I hope we can agree that we should concentrate on Afghanistan and not be tempted to launch any attacks on Iraq'. '**Absolutely**', replied Tenet.
The Times

Bush's warning was echoed by Sen. John McCain, a leading proponent of a troop increase. 'Is it going to be a strain on the military? **Absolutely**. Casualties are going to go up', the senator said.
Philadelphia Online

However, one person who will be coming is Pete's ex-wife Lynne. He added: 'Will Lynne be at the wedding? **Absolutely**. We still love each other, but just not in the way we did.
The Sun

You can avoid this overuse by answering 'yes' or, in the examples above, 'Yes, it is', 'Yes, we can', 'Yes, it is' and 'Yes, she will'.

actual *and* actually

The adjective **actual** and the adverb **actually** are overused in English, especially spoken English. In most cases, they add nothing to the meaning of what is being said.

Thomson said: 'We organise the CIS Cup but the **actual** decision on whether Kilmarnock could have used Hampden for training would have been up to Hampden Park Ltd'.

Daily Record

'I am [a fan], I admit guiltily. I don't care about the **actual** music. I like the really terrible people and watching Simon Cowell telling them they're rubbish.

Los Angeles Times

'The 20s are still for playing. By the time you turn 30 or 31, you can't turn around anymore, you're an **actual** adult. People get married later and later'.

Washington Times

She is still trying to assess where she stands in regards to in-your-face sexuality. 'I'm **actually** reading a book right now called *Female Chauvinist Pigs* [by Ariel Levy], which is really interesting to me because it shows both sides of it', says Pink.

Sydney Morning Herald

'Mickey does **actually** fall in love with Ian but the truth is, he'll do anything for sexual kicks'.

Daily Mirror

It is best to avoid using **actual** and **actually** unless they are needed to emphasize a contrast between what was expected and what in fact took place.

□ 39 □

awesome

The original meaning of **awesome** ('inspiring awe') has been overtaken in recent years by the slang meaning of 'amazing, great or impressive'.

> Since he has returned to his favoured position and come back from his eye problem of last season, Scholes has been **awesome**.
>
> *The Sun*

> In an online-only excerpt from her interview in *Rolling Stone*'s June 29th issue, the singer talks about Timbaland, gospel and her **awesome** high-school play.
>
> *Rolling Stone*

> 'It's one of those things you dream about', Cosgrove said of his introduction to international cricket. 'Just starting off with the first couple of runs took a weight off my shoulders, so to get 60-odd was pretty **awesome**'.
>
> *Sydney Morning Herald*

> 'That's the biggest win of the year so far', Francis said. 'Kasey did an **awesome** job driving tonight'.
>
> *Seattle Times*

> Stuart said: 'Kerry is an **awesome** talent and I for one would love to see her competing on a bigger stage'.
>
> *Daily Record*

Avoid **awesome** by using 'impressive', 'great' or 'excellent'.

basically

The adverb **basically** is often used in speech as a filler, adding nothing to the meaning.

'She was really choked up. She **basically** said how grateful she was for the support from all the staff', said Michael Hornby.
Sydney Morning Herald

The whole experience caused her to have a nervous breakdown. She said: '**Basically**, I wanted to commit suicide'.
Daily Record

She said: 'There were people queuing outside the practice at 7am, but lots of people didn't hear about it until later and were working anyway. It's ridiculous, I've **basically** got no dentist'.
The Herald

I didn't laugh any more, and friends would get embarrassed. And then I was embarrassed because they were embarrassed, so **basically** we stopped going out.
SHARON OSBOURNE *Extreme*

'We handed them the game, **basically**', said Renney, visibly agitated.
New York Post

Unless you are using **basically** to mean 'with reference to what is basic or fundamental', you should avoid it.

challenge

The noun **challenge** has accrued a range of meanings in recent years. In certain business environments, staff are urged to use **challenge** in place of the negative-sounding 'problem'. A **challenge** is also a task or job that has been allocated to someone. **Challenge** is used to describe any difficulty encountered. As a result, the word is overused.

'I have every confidence that Mr Watkins will ensure that the **challenges** are met', he said. 'He's able, experienced, a former police minister, successful'.

Sydney Morning Herald

Developing the show was a new **challenge** for Laliberte and director-writer Dominic Champagne. Cirque's previous shows have all been independently conceived, not based on any existing story or work.

Seattle Times

Last year England ended 16 years of hurt and won back the Ashes after the dramatic and decisive final Test at The Oval. Now, the ultimate **challenge** awaits as Andrew Flintoff 's men travel to Australia to retain the urn.

Daily Mail

'But the truth is that countryside everywhere is facing change and disruption over the next 100 years. It is going to be a **challenge** to all of us to manage that change'.

Daily Telegraph

Some alternatives to **challenge** include 'task', 'problem', 'job' and 'project'.

closure

It has become common to talk about **closure** in relation to events that occur within a person's life. In this context, **closure** is the sense of satisfaction or resignation felt when a particular episode comes to an end. Spreading from the specialist vocabulary of psychology into general language, the term **closure** is now greatly overused.

> The women say it is impossible to get **closure** until their questions are answered. In the meantime their anger remains fresh.
>
> *Daily Record*

> 'I need to see it for **closure**. I know he's gone, but in my heart I need to know what happened'.
>
> *G&M National*

> She had to confront them, find **closure** for her guilt, give them a chance to explain, so she could forgive them, and understand.
>
> Maree Giles *The Past is a Secret Country*

> Local fire company spokesman Mike Hart said the demolition of the building was 'a type of **closure**' for the community.
>
> *The Sun*

> Being given the opportunity for **closure** on his previously troubled relationship with Scotland is something David Weir is clearly cherishing.
>
> *The Herald*

You can use 'resolution', 'resignation' or 'satisfaction' in place of **closure** in some contexts.

dynamic

A **dynamic** is a moving or driving force that is instrumental in growth or change. It has also come to mean a relationship between people or organizations and, as such, occurs frequently.

> Meanwhile, Cronenberg lets the most interesting side of the story – the shifting **dynamic** between Jack, Edie and Tom – slip through his fingers.
>
> *The Herald*

> 'Whatever the strange **dynamic** of their relationship, Linda was the only one Paul could open up to', said Cox.
>
> *Sydney Morning Herald*

> The main interaction right now is a **dynamic** between Lebanon and Hizbullah, and whether it will remain an independent militia in a democratic country.
>
> *Christian Science Monitor*

> All three are represented by Perkins Coie, the Pacific Northwest's largest law firm. That must make for an interesting **dynamic** when the attorneys get together to share war stories.
>
> *Seattle P-I*

> If Strauss plays, it will not change the **dynamic** of how the team play in a match that pits English conformism against Sri Lankan unorthodoxy.
>
> *Daily Telegraph*

Instead of dynamic you can use 'relationship', 'connection' or 'communications'.

factor

A **factor** is an element in the composition of anything or in bringing about a certain result. It is often used as if it is a synonym of 'component' or 'part'.

'There's also an undeniable cool **factor** to boxing – always a paramount concern in LA'.

Los Angeles Times

The advice starts before consumers even enter their local wireless shop. It cites a number of **factors** to consider, including how much a user can afford to pay each month, how much airtime they'll need and what kind of wireless coverage is available.

G&M National

Food presentation is an important **factor** in food selection. Colour, flavour, texture and temperature are key ingredients in the successful presentation of food.

Sydney Morning Herald

Mr Bradshaw said the UK's pesticide regulation was amongst the toughest in the world. He also said pesticides were a necessary **factor** in the production of both organic and conventional food.

The Guardian

You can use 'component', 'element', 'part', 'feature' or 'constituent' in place of **factor**.

hopefully

Some people argue that **hopefully** can only mean 'in a hopeful manner', and that using it to mean 'it is to be hoped that' is incorrect. While most people are happy to use it to mean the latter, it is true that it is overused, especially in speech.

The 20-year-old said: 'It was brilliant for me and for the team. At the moment things are going well and **hopefully** they go as well in the next bit of the season'.

The Sun

'We will make recommendations, and **hopefully** Metro will implement them as soon as possible', he said.

Washington Times

'**Hopefully** this research will inspire a new approach to the treatment of Alzheimer's, one focused on preventing the loss of the brain cells instead of treating the resulting symptoms'.

Science Daily

'100 per cent support their call on the haka. **Hopefully** this will put an end to the clamour about it being nasty and intimidating'.

Rugby World

'I want to continue writing books and columns, to the end of my days **hopefully**'.

The Herald

In speech you can use 'I hope' instead of **hopefully**.

individual

An **individual** is a person. People often use **individual** in speech and writing when they are trying to convey a level of formality.

> UK citizens can log in and answer a series of questions about their personal spending habits. The calculator then applies price changes to the particular basket of goods and services purchased by that **individual**.
>
> *Sydney Morning Herald*

> The past 16 years have demonstrated to me what unpleasant **individuals** (all parties) we have elected to represent us in Parliament. With just a few exceptions, I would not welcome any of them as a colleague in my business life.
>
> *The Times*

> Many talented **individuals** are put off joining the technology sector, scared by the thought of joining a technical clique that relies on a complex language of codes and policies.
>
> *Computing UK*

> When combined with the library's collection of correspondence from Dietrich to Hemingway, these new letters help to complete the story of a remarkable friendship between two exceptional **individuals**.
>
> *The Guardian*

You should avoid using **individual** to mean a person, unless you want to emphasize the contrast between one single person and a number of people collectively. Use 'person' instead or, if appropriate, 'man' or 'woman'.

initiative

The **initiative** is the lead or first step in a process or plan. Through this meaning it has come to mean the process or plan itself, and this usage is overused.

> At its launch in October 2000, the scheme was billed as the biggest ever recruitment drive in Welsh sport – and it has exceeded all expectations. The **initiative** has attracted the support of world-renowned athletes such as Colin Jackson.
> *News Wales*

> I work closely with the power station on **initiatives** to clean rubbish along the beach in front of it.
> *BBC Magazine*

> In response to Israel's rejection of the **initiative**, Ghazi Hama, spokesman for the Hamas government, said Prime Minister Ehud Olmert was making a 'mistake'.
> *Jerusalem Post*

> 'And some of the skills and training **initiatives** proposed by the Scottish parliament are very positive, though they'll take time to work through'.
> *The Herald*

> Now Mr Blair has announced his Respect 'action plan' – the latest in a series of **initiatives** to crack down on yob culture.
> *Sydney Morning Herald*

You can avoid overuse of **initiative** by using 'plan', 'project' or 'scheme' instead.

joined-up

This is a relatively new adjective meaning 'coherent and coordinated'. It originated in political circles and has spread out from that rather limited sphere to the general language of the wider population.

'Tackling this issue requires a **joined-up** approach, which is why I am thrilled that the four police forces in Yorkshire are working together, alongside regional and national organisations to respond to this growing problem', Hollis said.

Computing UK

The move to allow Child Trust Fund money to roll over into an ISA when the holder reaches the age of 18 is a good example of **joined-up** government thinking.

Daily Telegraph

In a remarkable failure of **joined-up** policymaking, the government has killed off almost all central subsidies for mapmaking.

The Guardian

However, results can only be achieved by **joined-up** effort across government and across different sectors of our society.

Belfast Telegraph

George Hunter, director of Turning Point Scotland's Glasgow Drug Crisis Centre, says it will lead to a more **joined-up** service.

The Herald

Use 'coherent', 'coordinated', 'organized' or 'integrated' in place of **joined-up**.

journey

The noun **journey** has developed a new meaning in recent years. It is often used to describe a person's progress or course in their career or in some particular endeavour.

> As McDermott neared the end of his **journey** to reveal the lives behind the men of September 11, he was struck by two things.
>
> *The Herald*

> Gloucester's Heineken Cup **journey** is over but they went out with heads high after a pulsating tie during which they overhauled an early 14-point deficit.
>
> *Daily Telegraph*

> The past five years have been an **incredible journey** for us all – and having the original five back together was something that we had wanted to see happen for some time.
>
> *Daily Mirror*

> The team has played 24 Test series, drawn one and lost only two – in India in 2000-01 and last year's Ashes series in England. 'It's been an unbelievable **journey**', Buchanan said.
>
> *Sydney Morning Herald*

> The film will chart the It Girl's **journey** from art school student, to actress, to drug-addled mess.
>
> *Empire*

Depending on the context, you can use 'progress', 'career', 'development' or 'experience' instead of **journey**.

literally

Literally means 'using the literal, as opposed to the figurative, meaning of a word or phrase'. It is both overused and misused. When overused it is irritating and adds nothing to the meaning of what is being said. When misused it makes what is being said nonsensical, and distracts the reader or listener from the intended meaning.

'The guys have **literally** said this is one of the highlights of their 15 years of being together', said Field.

Sydney Morning Herald

'This year has been fantastic and instead of waking up and feeling sad, I **literally** wake up and feel so happy'.

Daily Record

In Tony Abbott's latest rant, he says 'for the unions, the next federal election is **literally** do or die'.

Sydney Morning Herald

History and its telling, quite **literally**, ran in Schlesinger's blood. His father, Arthur M. Schlesinger, was an immensely influential historian.

Sydney Morning Herald

Even as the South Africans and the pitches out there expose the inadequacies of the team, the selectors are **literally** rummaging through the cupboard of options back home.

Times of India

Retired Supreme Court Judge Gabriel Bach, whose family was **literally** kicked out of Germany by the Nazis before the start of the Second World War, will celebrate his 80th birthday in March.

Jerusalem Post

The safest thing to do is to avoid **literally** if at all possible.

nice

This adjective is very possibly the most overused word in the English language. Its use often indicates a lack of enthusiasm for whatever is under discussion, as well as a lack of imagination.

Moshe Rabbenu was a **nice** man.

Jerusalem Post

In high school, she made $6.25 a week cleaning houses so she could buy **nice** dresses and pay school club fees – all extra things she wanted for herself.

The News & Observer

Simons had all the trappings of success – a **nice** house, a boat and three children at private school.

Sydney Morning Herald

'Elizabeth was the **nicest** neighbour you could ever meet'.

Daily Record

'These are just ordinary people, they are not well-off and some of them are getting on, so they could do with the money, maybe to have a **nice** holiday before they die'.

Daily Telegraph

'Everyone comes here because the view is **nice**, and normally the air on the top of the bridge is cooler'.

Washington Times

There are numerous alternatives to **nice**, depending on the context: 'pleasant', 'agreeable', 'pleasurable', 'considerate', 'friendly', 'amiable', 'attractive', 'appealing' and 'fine' are just a few.

obviously

When used to modify a sentence, **obviously** means 'it is obvious that'. It is often used unnecessarily, where it adds nothing to the meaning of the sentence.

'Obviously it is disappointing not to win again but the progress we have made over the past few weeks has been enormous'.

Daily Record

'Our injuries are not ideal **obviously** but they are part and parcel of our sport and they will level out by the end of the season'.

Daily Telegraph

'Obviously we are thrilled and relieved that she has been released. We want to thank all that have supported and prayed for her'.

The Times

'We **obviously** have to solve the killings', he said.

Philadelphia Online

'Obviously everyone would like to get more publicity – OK, I would – but at this point in my career that's not my role'.

Seattle Times

'Lote would love to come back to Brisbane but **obviously** the Broncos would find it hard to find the money that he demands'.

Sydney Morning Herald

Try to avoid using **obviously** in this sense in your speech and writing.

on message *and* off message

In political language, someone who is **on message** is following the approved party line, while someone **off message** is not. These expressions are now used in general language.

> He's a scripted campaigner who stays **on message** and sometimes declines to provide a direct answer unless pushed.
> *Philadelphia Online*

> Afterwards, the Lions were all very much **on message**, claiming considerable satisfaction from a performance that had seen the best players from three national sides left 30 points adrift.
> *The Herald*

> No handling was needed. Ono stayed imperturbably **on message**, no matter what question she was asked. According to Ono, Lennon never cared about having hit records.
> *Los Angeles Times*

> Meanwhile, eager to discuss promising developments, Secretary of State Condoleezza Rice found herself knocked **off message**.
> *Seattle Times*

> Then, happily, he started to go **off message**. His early commercial activities, he explained, were driven by the need to buy recreational drugs.
> *The Economist*

> Even Padraig Harrington, who features in the advertisements for Fáilte Ireland, wandered **off message** on occasion.
> *The Guardian*

Try to avoid these phrases as they are overused to the point of cliché. You may have to rewrite your work to do this.

on stream

The literal meaning of **on stream** is 'coming into operation or production' or 'passing through a pipe or system'. The figurative sense, 'coming into being or practice, or becoming available', is now very common.

> The additional jobs will come **on stream** over three years and a high proportion will be high-skilled, requiring technical, electronic, research, sales and marketing qualifications.
>
> *RTE News Online*

> The captain's competitive juices are clearly already flowing, even if yesterday's shock 3-0 defeat by Hibernian points at the difficulty of keeping both domestic and European ambitions **on stream**.
>
> *The Herald*

> The film requires me to create an entirely new alien culture and language, and for that I want 'photo-real' CGI characters. Sophisticated enough performance-capture animation technology is only coming **on stream** now.
>
> *Total Film*

> Saltmarsh lamb comes **on stream** at the end of May and sells through to December while the Herdwick hoggs come in late winter and spring.
>
> *The Guardian*

This overused piece of example of jargon can be avoided by rewording, for example as 'Saltmarsh lamb becomes available at the end of May'.

own *and* ownership

In recent years the verb **own** has taken on a new meaning within business jargon. This is 'to take or have responsibility for'. By extension, **ownership** has taken on the meaning of 'responsibility'.

> The UK is currently in favour of a non-legislative approach where sport continues to **own** the problem of drug misuse and where governments work together to support the fight against doping in sport.
>
> *The Guardian*

> 'It will take a collaborative effort involving our criminal justice, corrections, legislative and human services community to fix the problem we are having with offenders on community supervision', Rahr said Thursday. 'We all **own this** issue'.
>
> *Seattle P-I*

> Delivering high-resolution video through a wireless connection, however, remains a daunting task, he cautioned. 'It sounds like they're taking **ownership** of the problem.'
>
> *Computing UK*

> Yes, an important reason to abolish capital punishment is that someone may be falsely accused. It may also be an easy way out for the individual who does not want to take **ownership** and face up to the committed crime.
>
> *Newsweek*

You can avoid these jargon words by using the simpler equivalents: 'be responsible for' or 'take responsibility for' and 'responsibility'.

package

The noun **package** is now used to describe a person with reference to the range of abilities and qualities they have or do not have. Someone who has all the attributes that are necessary for success in a particular field is or has **the complete, total** or **whole package**.

'We knew he wasn't the complete **package** when we brought him to Rangers but we told him there were aspects of his game that could be better'.

Daily Record

Franz Ferdinand made updated post-punk, clever pop music for the feet and the brain. The complete **package**.

Belfast Telegraph

'There's a good reason Alan rates him so highly', Waterhouse said yesterday. 'He's the complete **package** now that he's matured, and I am sure you'll see something quite special there on Saturday'.

Sydney Morning Herald

'He brings leadership. He knows how to win. He's the total **package**'.

The News & Observer

Larson became Lynne's manager and got his demo to Law at Universal Records. To Larson, Lynne is the total **package** – song-writing, voice and live show.

Philadelphia Online

Yesterday Becks was described by Miss World as the man she would choose as 'Mr World'. 'He has everything. The whole **package**. He has the figure, the look, the hair, everything'.

The Sun

This phrase is particularly overused in sports reporting.

quality

When used as an adjective, **quality** means 'of a high grade of excellence'. Used in many different contexts, it is particularly overused in sports reporting.

> The charity, which campaigns for accessible, affordable and **quality** child care, said parents must be given more financial help to meet growing costs.
>
> *Daily Telegraph*

> 'The reward for those of us that are in the elected leadership of the party is that we've had some really **quality** candidates step up'.
>
> *Washington Times*

> The government recently launched an action plan to close the gender pay gap. Creating more **quality** part-time roles is key to increasing the number of women in senior roles.
>
> *The Guardian*

> They need two more **quality** players for next season and they can make a real impact.
>
> *Sydney Morning Herald*

> She added: 'Labour should be about **quality** public services delivered by well-trained, well-respected public servants paid a fair wage'.
>
> *Daily Record*

> Ms Jowell told MPs she wants the BBC to raise its game and produce more **quality** shows like The Office and Bleak House.
>
> *The Sun*

Alternatives to **quality** include 'excellent', 'first-class', 'first-rate', 'exceptional' and 'superior'.

□ 58 □

scenario

Scenario has come to mean 'any imagined or suggested plan of action or sequence of events'. A popular jargon word, it is often used in sentences where it adds nothing to the meaning.

His dream **scenario** would be a place in the final of the Commonwealth Bank Series – an achievement that would confirm his status as the team's saviour.

Daily Telegraph

Given that this is a **scenario** that has occurred on a number of successive years we call upon the Government to ensure construction projects are procured in good time.

Belfast Telegraph

'When the interest rate **scenario** changes, we would review our decision', the official added.

Times of India

The problems we face in Iraq are large but we should note that the civil war **scenario** simply hasn't taken place. Nor has Iraq been destroyed.

Newsweek

Police, ambulance crews and fire-fighters took over Murrayfield stadium in Edinburgh for a mock poison gas attack **scenario**.

The Herald

Sony said: 'We want stock to be freely available at launch and on an ongoing basis, thereby avoiding the boom and bust **scenarios** normally associated with hardware launches'.

The Guardian

In each of these examples, **scenario** could be removed without any meaning being lost.

situation

The noun **situation** is often used where it is quite
unnecessary. When it follows another noun, it is often
redundant.

'It's the most interesting business turnaround **situation** I
have found in two years of looking around for interesting and
exciting opportunities', he says.

Sydney Morning Herald

Roeder is adamant that the lifesaving operation he underwent
in the summer of 2003 has made him the perfect man for the
crisis **situation** in which he now finds himself.

Daily Mirror

'When the British team won medals in Germany last month, it
included girls that MacLarty had previously beaten. Australia
showed she has come of age in handling pressure **situations**.

The Herald

Its style is usually to invest in a company alongside the
management, and it does not want to damage its reputation by
getting involved in a hostile bid **situation**.

Belfast Telegraph

The percentage of dentists who reported child-abuse
situations to appropriate authorities increased to 73.1 percent
in 1997 from 1994's 62.2 percent.

Science Daily

Even as women are proving their mettle in combat **situations**,
they often, like men, face adjustments when they return to the
US or to civilian life.

Christian Science Monitor

The word **situation** is unnecessary in each of these citations.

synergy

This has to be one of the most overused jargon words of recent years, a favourite in business language, and one that seems more often used to impress than to convey meaning.

> He believes there are **synergies** to be gained from a merger between radio and television stations but not between newspapers and electronic media.
>
> *Sydney Morning Herald*

> 'Our economies are complementary. We have to improve **synergy** and speed up the overall development'.
>
> *Times of India*

> Chin said the four-day event would help to identify new areas of **synergy** between palm oil and the snack food industry, which could be developed into a vast market.
>
> *Daily Express*

> The **synergy** between the two men is underpinned by a sense of mutual trust and an almost instinctive anticipation of how each will react in a given set of circumstances.
>
> *The Guardian*

> The broker said: 'A merger between EMI and Warner would add very significant value, both in terms of cost **synergies** and increased scale'.
>
> *Belfast Telegraph*

There may be occasions on which **synergy** is the word you need, but beware of using it simply to impress, as its use can suggest the speaker is someone who pretends to know more than they really do.

time bomb

In its figurative sense, a **time bomb** is a set of circumstances that will develop into a serious problem unless action is taken immediately.

> Global warming is creating a climate **time bomb** by storing enormous amounts of heat in the waters of the north Atlantic, UK scientists have discovered.
> *The Guardian*

> Experts have warned that Britain is facing a health **time bomb** as the number of binge drinkers continues to rise.
> *Daily Mirror*

> The response is an attempt to change children's eating habits and defuse the 'ticking **time bomb**' of obesity among Scotland's young people.
> *The Herald*

> With more than a quarter of the current nursing workforce due to retire by 2021, a pay cut would do nothing to tackle the retirement **time bomb** currently facing the NHS.
> *The Sun*

> London may be facing a property **time bomb** with the average house price in the capital forecast to reach £400,000 in five years' time, experts warned today.
> *The Guardian*

> 'The obesity epidemic is surging and people don't realize they're setting themselves up to develop diabetes. They're like ticking **time bombs**', said Dr Manisha Chandalia.
> *Science Daily*

This figurative sense is so overused it is best to avoid it.

tragedy *and* tragic

In its original meaning, a **tragedy** was a drama dealing with disastrous events involving the fall of an honourable, worthy and important person. The meaning expanded to become any disaster or sad event, especially one involving death or killing. It is now used often to describe an event that is simply unfortunate, uncomfortable or even disappointing. This is also true of its related adjective **tragic**.

> 'He's one of the form players', Berrigan said. 'He's on fire. It'd be a **tragedy** if he didn't get picked for the Anzac Test'.
>
> *Sydney Morning Herald*

> One of the listed locations is Hammersmith Palais, the west London nightclub, which now faces the threat of demolition. 'It's a **tragedy** that it's going', Mr McNicholas said.
>
> *The Guardian*

> 'Glamour is gone, which is a little **tragic**', she says. 'I go to Catholic Mass, and I'm appalled – people are wearing sweat clothes to church.
>
> *New York Post*

> 'As things stand, it's not just current England players that won't be released, it's any Premiership player. It's **tragic** that it looks as if we might head into next season with the same old problems'.
>
> *Daily Telegraph*

If you are about to use **tragedy** or **tragic**, think of this: does your story involve the fall of a once-great person, or premature or violent death? If not, then perhaps 'sad', 'shocking', 'disappointing', 'regrettable' or 'unfortunate' are more appropriate.

tsar *or* czar

A **tsar** is a person who has been appointed an authority or adjudicator on some subject. The number of **tsars** appointed in recent years has led to some criticism and much ridicule of the term.

> Mr Blair's anti-social behaviour **tsar** Louise Casey said bad parents should be forced to take courses to control kids.
>
> *Daily Mirror*

> Paul Haggis is developing Against All Enemies, a drama based on the memoirs of former counter-terrorism **tsar** Richard Clarke.
>
> *Sydney Morning Herald*

> The drug is cheaper than cocaine or heroin – as little as $20 per gram, according to a report from the drug **czar**'s office.
>
> *Newsweek*

> Jamie Oliver wants to be the first food **tsar** and to work for free. He wants to lead a team of advisers to make Brits less fat and better fed.
>
> *Daily Mirror*

> Forestry bosses are echoing the famous Monty Python sketch about a cross-dressing lumberjack. They are advertising for a diversity **tsar** – to recruit gay and transsexual lumberjacks.
>
> *Daily Record*

> The report, Commercialisation of Childhood, comes amid a national inquiry by the Children's Society into childhood conducted by the Government's unofficial 'happiness **tsar**' Lord Layard.
>
> *Daily Telegraph*

Avoid **tsar** by using 'expert', 'authority' or 'adviser' instead.

witch hunt

It has become common for any kind of investigation or review of a practice, policy or occurrence to be described as a **witch hunt**. This implies that the purpose of the examination is to find a likely-looking culprit to blame and punish publicly, while the true motive of the search is political, and often, concealed. The accuracy of this description depends on your standpoint, but what is not debatable is the overuse of **witch hunt**.

Close colleagues claim she is the victim of a **witch hunt**, and denied there had been any proved conflict of interest.

The Guardian

Academics last night condemned as a **witch hunt** a student campaign to oust an Oxford don because of his links to an immigration watchdog.

Daily Telegraph

Mr Lay, who slammed the investigation as a **witch hunt** during the trial, is the most high-profile corporate executive to be targeted by the Justice Department.

Seattle Times

The president has vehemently denied the allegations, which surfaced last summer, declaring himself the victim of a **witch hunt**.

Jerusalem Post

Indeed, last week's **witch hunt** of a mother with an overweight child shows what social services think about families.

Spiked

Alternatives to **witch hunt** include 'persecution' and 'victimization'.

and so on and so forth

This phrase, which means 'and more of the same or the like', has become clichéd.

> The messiah is coming. There is a well-known scenario of the course of events, the battle of Gog and Magog **and so on and so forth**. There is a final struggle ending with the final victory.
>
> *Jerusalem Post*

> He didn't like New York: materialistic, mechanistic, trivial, idolatrous, wanton, depraved, **and so on and so forth**. Washington was a little better.
>
> *The Guardian*

> If Hezbollah hits Tel Aviv, for example, Israel could kick its campaign up a notch and hit Syria or even Iran. Then Iran's Shiite supporters in Iraq could start another insurgency, **and so on and so forth**.
>
> *The Slate*

> 'Well, I anticipate during the course of this trial you will have, as it were, a free short tuition in what poker is all about, what poker involves, how it works **and so on and so forth**'.
>
> *The Times*

> 'Veal with orange. It's got all sorts in it. Stoned raisins, currants, nutmeg, oranges, **and so on and so forth**'.
>
> EMMA BLAIR *Three Bites of the Cherry*

Avoid it by using 'and the like' or 'and the rest of it' instead.

at the end of the day

This cliché is enormously popular, appearing in contexts as varied as politics and sport. Its purpose is to introduce a summation or conclusion.

'The whole situation is a nightmare – I've lost my husband, my daughter and my granddaughter all in one go', says Susan. Yet incredibly, she has forgiven Lisa, saying '**At the end of the day**, she's still my daughter'.

Daily Mirror

As one in his circle confides: 'Pete is a junkie, and **at the end of the day** all that matters to him is where he scores his drugs'.

Daily Mail

'We are an organisation set up at the request of the prime minister in 2000 to consider all aspects of food safety. We can advise, but **at the end of the day** it will be up to ministers to make decisions'.

The Herald

All three have since been released on bail and are living in England. Victor said: '**At the end of the day**, the truth about what happened that day is going to come out in court.

Belfast Telegraph

All these examples would retain their meaning if **at the end of the day** were omitted. It could be replaced by 'ultimately' or 'in the end' but it is not necessary.

at this moment in time

Given that a moment is a point of time, it is unnecessary to add 'in time' after 'at this moment'. Nevertheless, this cliché is widespread, especially in the language of sport.

'I'm obviously keen to enter management at some stage but **at this moment in time** I'm a player and will be here until the end of the season. We'll see what comes about after that'.
Daily Record

'Although unity is important, it is not the most important value I think it is a tribute to the Democratic Party **at this moment in time** that we are honestly and openly struggling with a lot of difficult issues facing our country'.
Washington Times

'It is not very sensible **at this moment in time** to send a signal of weakness', refusing to rule out the military option, saying Britain should instead 'send a signal of strength'.
Jerusalem Post

'I will be either over the moon or upset but, as long as we have a good performance on Friday, that's all that really matters to me **at this moment in time**'.
Daily Mail

Avoid it by using 'at this moment', 'just now' or 'right now'.

be the new

This linguistic formula is so clichéd that it has its own dedicated column in the magazine *Private Eye*. Reflecting the relentless quest for 'the next big thing', this convention is seen as a handy shortcut for explaining some new trend or product by comparing it to something already familiar. The examples that follow give an idea of the astonishing spread of this cliché.

In magazine land the 'green issue' **is the new** 'sex issue'.
Sydney Morning Herald

If Toronto **is the new** Florence, Vancouver **is the new** Venice.
G&M National

Dan Carter **is the new** Jonny Wilkinson.
The Guardian

She might have also said: 'Breakfast **is the new** lunch'.
The Times

Paella **is the new** pie and mash.
The Herald

'Cider', says the Guardian, '**is the new** chardonnay'.
BBC Magazine

Serrano ham **is the new** prosciutto di Parma.
Newsweek

'Ubiquity **is the new** exclusivity'.
The News & Observer

60 **is the new** 40.
Philadelphia Online

cause a headache

This cliché means 'to cause a problem'.

> The situation is **causing massive headaches** in the plan to replace the patched-up Sea Kings by early 2009.
>
> *G&M National*

> Inadequate planning for the UK's upcoming recycling law may **cause legal headaches** for firms.
>
> *Computing UK*

> Catastrophic events such as the Buncefield explosion or the Kensal Rise tornado are thankfully rare, but even the more mundane household damage claims can **cause major headaches** for those involved.
>
> *Daily Telegraph*

> His form this season has been outstanding, which will be welcomed by Queensland selectors but may **cause a giant headache** for Australian selectors who must pick a team this week for the Anzac Test against New Zealand.
>
> *Sydney Morning Herald*

> The bill **caused a major headache** for Tony Blair, who faced a bitter backbench revolt from as many as 100 rebel Labour MPs.
>
> *The Guardian*

> 'A victory in Tel Aviv would be perfect for us', said Bilic. 'I believe my players will display their best and we'll do all we can to **cause a severe headache** for the Israeli side on Wednesday night'.
>
> *Jerusalem Post*

You can avoid this by replacing **headache** with 'problem' or 'difficulty'.

come to terms with

If you **come to terms with** a personal difficulty or problem, you find a way of living with it. This expression is popular in the media, and you will often hear it used in relation to grieving families and classmates in the wake of sudden or violent deaths, as well as in other, less dramatic contexts.

It's a devastating day for the school community. Everybody is in grief and shock and we are all trying to **come to terms with** the tragedy.

Sydney Morning Herald

The former Beatle confessed he is struggling to **come to terms with** the break-up of their four-year marriage.

Daily Record

We must first **come to terms with** being champions and that every team will raise their game to beat us.

The Sun

The early 1990s were dark days for the music business establishment, which had not **come to terms with** the dance revolution that began a few years earlier.

Belfast Telegraph

That is the word from midfielder Jarrad McVeigh, who is still **coming to terms with** the gut-wrenching one-point loss to West Coast at the MCG last September.

Sydney Morning Herald

You can use verbs like 'cope' and 'accept' in order to avoid this cliché.

cool, calm and collected

This expression has become something of a cliché. Its overuse is probably due in part to the alliteration.

> She attributes her success to her **'cool, calm and collected demeanour '**, which never falters – even when she is faced with death threats.
>
> *The Guardian*

> But as quickly as it happened, it was over, and Sam was back to his **cool, calm, collected** self.
>
> PETER GURALNICK *Dream Boogie*

> Beckenbauer, Germany's tournament ambassador, was a World Cup winner as a player and manager and arguably the most stylish defender the game has ever seen. He was **cool, calm and collected**. Nothing ever ruffled him.
>
> *The Sun*

> She sits down suddenly on the stool before the vanity and looks at herself in the glass. She's **cool, calm and collected**. No tears, no hysterics, no panic.
>
> SUSAN HOWATCH *Sins of the Fathers*

> 'I'd like to tell you that I'm **calm, cool and collected** about it all, but I haven't been able to sleep – not with anxiety, but in anticipation of it all happening.
>
> *Sydney Morning Herald*

Avoid this by using 'cool' or 'calm' or 'collected' individually.

emotional rollercoaster

An **emotional rollercoaster** is used to describe an event which has caused the speaker to feel a range of conflicting emotions such as elation and depression, anxiety and anticipation, or hope and despair.

> 'It was all tied up with a few hours to spare but the last 24 hours have been an **emotional rollercoaster**. Thankfully it has all ended positively and I couldn't be more delighted'.
>
> *Daily Record*

> The presentation of this utterly original book presents a challenge: how to convey the literary sophistication and **emotional rollercoaster** as well as the broad comedy of the characters?
>
> *The Guardian*

> Looking into her family history was an **emotional rollercoaster** for the 69-year-old, who found herself reduced to tears as the TV show discovered that her great-great-grandfather had died a pauper in the workhouse.
>
> *Daily Mirror*

> 'We all celebrated, then we had to kick-start our internal farm economy – all of these things are part of the **emotional rollercoaster** of farming.
>
> *Sydney Morning Herald*

> Jacqueline, 46, tells of her **emotional rollercoaster** of three failed IVF attempts.
>
> *The Sun*

Avoid this phrase if possible. You can describe an experience or event as 'difficult', 'emotional' or 'trying'.

hold one's hands up

If you say that you **hold your hands up**, it means that you are admitting responsibility for a mistake or misdeed you have made. This expression is often accompanied by the physical gesture.

Vaughan said: 'I fully understand why they have given us that sort of reception. We have to **hold our hands up** and accept all the criticism that comes our way'.

Sydney Morning Herald

'The first goal was always going to be crucial and I **hold my hands up**. It was my mistake and in a way it cost us the game'.

Daily Telegraph

She said: 'My behaviour was wrong and I **hold my hands up**. I apologise to Shilpa's parents. It's not nice because I wouldn't want to see my daughter go through that'.

Daily Mirror

Attempts to explain to British Gas that this bill wasn't her mother's proved fruitless, so Mrs Bell contacted us again at the end of January. Yet again, British Gas **held its hands up** and admitted the problem was on its side.

The Guardian

I have to **hold my hands up** and concede that I did not choose the right team.

GORDON STRACHAN *Strachan*

in a very real sense

This is a cliché that adds nothing to a statement. In the following citations, **in a very real sense** can be deleted without any sense being lost.

'**In a very real sense**, cold-related illnesses are a very British disease. We know the hardship that older people face in the winter'.

New Wales

In a very real sense, Saddam Hussein, along with various other dictators in that region, was a product of US and British foreign policy: brought to power with the help of the CIA in 1979 and thereafter enjoying the support of British and US governments for most of his time in power.

The Herald

With immigration becoming such a pivotal issue, people need to remember that **in a very real sense** immigration is what keeps us growing and helps invigorate our society in myriad ways.

Time

'I don't think we can put barriers on the march of a nation. **In a very real sense**, we are in the process of independence'.

Daily Record

Nobody rated his chances of pulling off the amazing rescue job to stop the Pars from exiting the SPL, so **in a very real sense** there was no great pressure on him for this end-of-season fixture.

The Herald

in actual fact

In fact means 'actually', therefore there is no need to insert 'actual' into this phrase. Nevertheless, **in actual fact** is commonly used.

> 'I'm getting a little bored with everyone going on about Toyota's hybrid Prius. Yes, it has lots of clever technology and is, of course, a worthy effort. But **in actual fact**, it's not that economical and takes an awful lot of energy to build because there are so many systems in it'.
>
> *Daily Mirror*

> 'They may choose to carry a weapon for a variety of reasons, whether it's fear or fashion. Although some think they are making themselves safer, they can **in actual fact** be much more vulnerable'.
>
> *Daily Record*

> In theory, this process should take more than three hours before clouds become 'ripe' enough to release rain, whereas **in actual fact** it takes only half an hour or so.
>
> *Science Daily*

> Wiggins' team manager at Cofidis, Eric Boyer, feels that **in actual fact** his protégé does not yet have sufficient belief in his own ability. 'Brad is a super rider but he needs to gain in confidence', said Boyer.
>
> *The Guardian*

> 'But **in actual fact** it takes a lot of hard work to make something look easy'.
>
> *The Sun*

Avoid **in actual fact** by using 'in fact', 'in truth' or 'actually'.

in the shop window

A cliché from the world of sport that has moved into general language, a person who is or has put himself or herself **in the shop window** is trying to demonstrate their abilities and experience in the hope of getting another, better job.

'There'll be a British final and then there's two semis and a final in Sweden and you can qualify from that. I'm also **in the shop window** as there will be riders picked for the GPs by invitation'.

The Sun

Although we had said we would not allow the player to go on loan anywhere else, we decided it was in our best interests to let him move to a Premiership club where he will be **in the shop window**.

The Herald

Mr Sharon's central role in the campaign is not purely a matter of spin. By keeping him **in the shop window**, his political heirs hope to associate themselves with the big idea that transformed the last years of Mr Sharon's long and controversial career.

Sydney Morning Herald

'Money doesn't motivate me and I have never put myself **in the shop window**', he said. 'Opportunities have just come my way, and I guess I've been able to recognise them when they do come'.

The Herald

move the goalposts

Another sporting idiom that has entered general language, **move the goalposts** is well established as a cliché in English. It can refer to any unfair changing of conditions after an agreement has been made.

> Many Palestinians believe that European governments, in particular, have **moved the goalposts** in refusing to accept Hamas's victory in democratic elections until it formally recognises Israel.
>
> *The Times*

> 'This is an example of worst practice and is typical of the way Banco Santander have managed Abbey since they bought it. They have been continually **moving the goalposts** at the expense of staff morale and job security, which can only have a knock-on effect on customer service'.
>
> *The Herald*

> But Britain – unfairly and without warning – **moved the immigration goalposts** after that, the affected Indians said.
>
> *Times of India*

> 'Tony Blair is always saying that people need to be more entrepreneurial and business minded. But how are farmers supposed to achieve this when the government keeps **moving the goalposts**?
>
> *News Wales*

> 'That was my task and that was what I was working towards, but unfortunately the **goalposts were moved**'.
>
> *Daily Record*

not be rocket science

Any activity that is considered by the speaker to be easy or requiring little intelligence can be described as **not rocket science**. A person considered to be of limited intelligence can be described as **not a rocket scientist**. These clichés have become hugely popular in recent years.

I ought to know how a restaurant works. After all, it **is hardly rocket science**.

The Times

'You reach the stage where you go to hotels expecting to be disappointed. I travel without high expectations. It just needs to be clean rooms and friendly service. **It's not rocket science**.

The Herald

The concept itself was not radical. Retail **has never been rocket science**: you buy an item from your supplier at one price, you sell it at a margin.

Sydney Morning Herald

'Drummers', he observes, 'aren't **rocket scientists**'.

The Herald

Home-cooked meals, clean clothes and a fully-stocked fridge. It doesn't take a **rocket scientist** to work out the benefits for most people of living with their parents.

BBC Magazine

Boothroyd said: 'It doesn't take a **rocket scientist** to work out that we've got to score more goals. We're competing but not winning games'.

The Sun

on the line

If something, such as your reputation or your career, is **on the line**, it is at risk of ending or being ruined.

'Ah, the hell with it!' I said suddenly, knowing my whole survival was **on the line** and grabbing every ounce of nerve I still possessed.

SUSAN HOWATCH *Sins of the Fathers*

But there are limits and so I told Jessie to shut up in no uncertain terms. It was my life **on the line**, not hers, and she had no business to talk to me as though she had never done anything wrong in her life.

ANNABEL GOLDSMITH *Copper: A Dog's Life*

He knows that England's honour is **on the line** here and that if England stumble in Israel it will be an earthquake in football.

Daily Telegraph

The Hollywood hell-raiser's career is now **on the line** as a result of her reputation.

The Sun

Do you know someone who deserves to be thanked? Remember all those men and women who put their lives **on the line** every day, not just the life-savers and action heroes.

Daily Record

outpouring of grief

It seems now to be expected that the death of any public figure, or of any person in particularly distressing circumstances, will be followed by what is almost invariably described as an **outpouring of grief**.

> When he died of cancer in 1948, at the age of 53, it triggered an **outpouring of grief** more commonly associated with a beloved political figure or religious leader. More than 200,000 people filed past his coffin as he lay in state at Yankee Stadium.
>
> *Belfast Telegraph*

> The Sun website was flooded with tributes after his shock death in September. In a global **outpouring of grief**, more than 20,000 readers signed our online book of condolences – the biggest response ever.
>
> *The Sun*

> Pope John Paul II's death prompted a remarkable **outpouring of grief** and respect from admirers of all faiths.
>
> *Seattle Times*

> In the fevered week after the death of Diana, Princess of Wales, the Queen was abused by tabloid papers for not responding quickly enough to the wide, if shallow, **outpouring of grief** that convulsed parts of the country.
>
> *Daily Telegraph*

This journalistic cliché should be avoided.

own goal

Extended from the football meaning, an **own goal** is a move that turns out to the disadvantage of the party making it.

Friends of the Earth said: It has scored an **own goal** by allowing aviation to expand'.

Daily Mirror

Mr Gove claimed that Labour had 'scored an **own goal** by using the World Cup to bury their bad news'.

Daily Telegraph

Developers have been zealous in their creation of new hotels to cash in on the crowds the World Cup will inevitably bring But could this ultimately be an **own goal** for German hoteliers?

The Guardian

He has won three terms in office for the Labour Party and probably would have won a fourth term if he had not scored a ruinous **own goal** by saying he would stand down for Gordon Brown before the next election.

The Herald

'This would be an **own goal** by those organisations who say they want to cut vehicle pollution'.

Belfast Telegraph

Centrica, the owner of British Gas, scored an astounding PR **own goal** yesterday. It hiked its dividend to shareholders by 22 per cent – exactly the same amount by which British Gas raised its prices last Friday.

The Sun

pay tribute to

The idiom **pay tribute to** means 'to acknowledge gratitude to or admiration for a person or thing'. Strictly, you **pay tribute to** someone who has made an important contribution to society, or whose achievements are significant. In recent years, **pay tribute to** has become confused with 'pay respects to' or 'pay one's final respects to', which means 'to show one's sadness at the death of'. Hence, we read reports of people **paying tribute to** a young child who has died, instead of 'paying their respects to'.

He **paid tribute to** 'a great kid', saying: 'I've heard of his moneymaking schemes, I've seen his infectious smile'.
Daily Mirror

In this town of more than 60 nationalities, Sikh turbans mixed with more sombre Christian colours of mourning as the community came together to **pay tribute to** its lost son.
Sydney Morning Herald

The man, who lost his wife 18 months ago, said the site gave him a chance to **pay tribute to** her. 'It just gives you some peace', he said. 'I feel she is closer to me when I am on the site'.
The Guardian

Hundreds gathered to **pay tribute to** the youngsters who died when the car they were travelling in left the road.
The Herald

poisoned chalice

A **poisoned chalice** is an apparent gift or benefit that is likely to cause great trouble to the recipient. This cliché is often used to describe a new job or promotion.

> As **poisoned chalices** go, the leadership of the Liberal Democrats 12 months ago resembled something rustled up by Lucrezia Borgia on one of her more vengeful days.
>
> *The Economist*

> It is unlikely to have come as a particularly welcome submission for the police chief , who is now in charge of one of the most politically sensitive operations that the Yard has ever undertaken – and a **poisoned chalice** if ever there was one.
>
> *Daily Telegraph*

> 'I knew there was only one way out of Wigan and that was the sack. The Wigan job has become a **poisoned chalice** and it'll be interesting to see who takes it on next'.
>
> *Daily Mirror*

> Almost every coach in Australia has been linked with the position, which has fast become the sport's most **poisoned chalice**.
>
> *Sydney Morning Herald*

> You could argue that the Mercury Music Prize is a **poisoned chalice**. Just ask Ms Dynamite, Pulp, Suede, Badly Drawn Boy ... and Gomez. After career-defining albums got the nod from judges, their careers seemed to go in reverse.
>
> *The Sun*

push the envelope

If you **push the envelope**, you try to achieve more than seems possible. It is sometimes used as an alternative for 'push the boundaries'.

Recently, the Forest Rights Bill was passed, giving more power to the grassroots to preserve forests even as they earn from it. The trend of civil society **pushing the envelope** on environmental issues in our cities has also worked wonders.

Times of India

'This is a good thing for the online retail industry; Tesco is **pushing the envelope** and forcing the competition to step up and compete', he argued.

Computing UK

'This is really **pushing the envelope** in how small you can go with these channels and still have a working device', Mudawar said.

Science Daily

Cameron is a famously hard-working and intense film-maker renowned for **pushing the envelope**.

The Guardian

From its composite fuselage and wings, to the revolutionary way that some critical systems are electrically powered, The Boeing Co has **pushed the technology envelope** with its 787 Dreamliner.

Seattle P-I

Murdoch's people finally developed the FX cable network and started investing heavily in smart, innovative programming, **pushing the envelope** in terms of language, violence and nudity.

The Guardian

set one's stall out

To **set your stall out** is to make clear from the outset what your intentions are.

> 'I'm not prepared to change my schedule just for one week's golf', he said. 'I **set my stall out** last year to play in America and I'm going to stick to it'.
>
> *Daily Mirror*

> He is adamant he won't abandon his passing philosophy and believes **setting his stall out** defensively at home would be testament to sacrilege. He said: 'The unwritten rule in football is you don't stay behind the ball and defend'.
>
> *Daily Record*

> In the early months of 2005, after his first resignation, the former home secretary, in his own words '**set my stall out** to come back into government'. His tactics worked, and he returned as work and pensions secretary after the May 2005 election.
>
> *Daily Telegraph*

> 'Last time, I made the mistake of trying to come back too soon and I **set my stall out** to do that and I did not see the dangers coming', he says. 'I am not going to make that mistake again'.
> *The Guardian*

You can avoid this cliché by using 'to make one's aims (or intentions) clear'.

sing from the same hymn sheet

This idiom, meaning 'to be in or be seen to be in agreement with another person', is becoming increasingly clichéd.

'He's a confident sort of player and his understanding of the game is very good. We **sing from the same hymn sheet** in terms of how we want to play the game.

The Guardian

'We want to make sure that both us and our vendors are **singing from the same hymn sheet** when it comes to the retail market', he added.

Computing UK

'They're really **singing off the same hymn sheet**', says one adviser who has been closely involved in at least the last eight budgets. 'You'd be amazed at how similar their views are'.

Sydney Morning Herald

Contrary to widely expressed fears that Condoleezza Rice would **sing to the neoconservatives' hymn sheet**, the new US secretary of state left Europe last week with glowing reports.

The Herald

'Some do really take it seriously and others don't. They are all **singing from different hymn sheets**'.

Disability Now

It is worth rewording your writing or speech in order to avoid using this cliché.

space of time

There is no need for the 'space of' in the phrase **space of time**. It is an unnecessary addition, which does nothing more than pad out whatever is being said.

> The Fine Gael Spokeswoman on Education, Olwyn Enright, said that what was of particular concern was that the accident was the second serious one to involve a school bus in such a short **space of time**.
>
> *RTE News Online*

> The roads, even in the short **space of time** in which Helen had been at Julia's flat, had grown almost empty.
>
> SARAH WATERS *The Night Watch*

> Two seconds elapsed, and it was during this extraordinarily brief **space of time** that Jack gave me that look, one I'd never seen before. I couldn't turn away.
>
> *Newsweek*

> All the major life-changing events, like getting engaged, planning a wedding and having a baby, have happened to me in such a short **space of time** that I'm still catching my breath.
>
> *Belfast Telegraph*

> Lovebox, held in east London last weekend, is an example of how the festival menu has changed in a relatively short **space of time**. Burgers and chips were notable by their absence this year.
>
> *The Guardian*

Replacing **space of time** with **time** would work perfectly well in the above examples.

step up to the plate

This American idiom, originating from baseball, has also become surprisingly well established as a cliché in British English. It means 'to put oneself forward in order to take on new responsibility'.

Governments have to **step up to the plate** and to step in with legislation when it is needed; giving all the responsibility to markets and consumers is not good enough.

BBC News

'With this astonishing level of food deprivation in America', Brown concluded, 'we need President Bush to **step up to the plate**. If he now asks Congress to cut federal food programs, hunger will increase even further'.

Science Daily

He said: 'We need families, communities and individuals to **step up to the plate** and to understand it is not just about stopping the bad things, it is about actively doing the good things'.

Daily Mail

Having **stepped up to the plate** for Scotland on several occasions, and having performed with real credit almost every time, it must be frustrating for Ross that he has not been given the credit he deserves.

The Herald

'Hopefully we can **step up to the plate** and raise our game against Ecuador'.

Daily Record

□ 89 □

take one's eye off the ball

This sporting idiom has moved into general language, and developed the meaning 'to become distracted from one's original task or aim'.

> 'But **they took their eye off the ball**, spent a fortune on a new headquarters and built up a disastrous internet and call centre business when they should have been concentrating on quality and service'.
>
> *The Herald*

> Mr Iemma denied **he had taken his eye off the ball** on gang crime in the south-west.
>
> *Sydney Morning Herald*

> 'The Bush administration **took its eye off the ball** in Afghanistan, leaving a deteriorating situation to worsen and Osama bin Laden on the loose more than five years after 9/11', said Democratic National Committee Press Secretary Stacie Paxton.
>
> *Washington Times*

> 'Revenues will not materialise until the next decade, but suppliers can't afford **to take their eye off the ball** today if they want to stay in the game', added O'Brien.
>
> *Computing UK*

> Healthcare Commission chief executive Anna Walker added: 'This Trust **took its eye off the patient safety ball**'.
>
> *Daily Mirror*

You can avoid this cliché by using 'lose focus' or 'lose sight of one's priorities'.

the bottom line

The bottom line in any situation is its most important aspect. This sense has developed from the financial meaning of **bottom line**: the final line on a financial statement, showing net profit or loss.

'We try our best to be compassionate, but **the bottom line** is we need to be firm with this opting-out policy and respect the wishes of the dead', he said.

Daily Telegraph

The Washington University trauma team continues to look for better ways to treat burn patients. '**The bottom line** is that so many of these accidents are preventable', Foglia says.

Science Daily

John E Healy, the co-chair of Archmere's capital campaign, said **the bottom line** was the wellbeing of the students.

Philadelphia Online

The real price of your home is what somebody is willing to pay for it – that's **the bottom line**.

Newsweek

And while charm helps pay the bills, it only goes so far: **the bottom line** is that the ferry service is expensive to run and used by hardly anybody.

Sydney Morning Herald

'Health workers are not disinfecting their hands as often as they should', he said. 'That is **the bottom line**'.

Belfast Telegraph

they think it's all over – it is now

The 1966 World Cup final between England and West Germany provided one of the great clichés of our time. In the dying seconds of the game, the commentator Kenneth Wolstonholme, observing fans on the pitch, declared 'They think it's all over ... It is now'. This sentence has now become so entrenched in British English that it can be abbreviated (as in the BBC TV programme *They Think It's All Over*) or adapted (as in the second example below) and the listener or reader still understands its connotations. It is much beloved of journalists, as the following examples show.

As German shoulders slumped, Del Piero was fed by Gilardino, two substitutes combining for the killer blow. They **thought it was all over**. It was.

The Times

They think the construction's all over, it is now – but only in Lego. This scale model of Wembley was built in just three weeks at a cost of £1,000. It is two feet wide and has 10,000 bricks.

The Sun

They think it's all over. But a host of Afghan challenges remain.

The Guardian

The final now goes to Cardiff's Millennium Stadium for the sixth successive year. A Wembley source said yesterday: '**They thought it was all over – it is now**. The cost of the project may now top £1billion following contract disputes, technical problems and poor weather'.

The Sun

think outside the box

When someone **thinks outside the box**, they disregard conventional thinking in order to achieve an original solution to a problem. This is good example of business jargon that has become general language cliché.

'As far as coaching's concerned, I'm still forward-thinking, I can **think outside of the box** and I can get to basics. I think I can cover the full spectrum'.

Daily Telegraph

When it comes to transport in the 21st century, we need not only to **think outside the box** but maybe also to sit inside the box and have it dragged along by huskies.

The Times

'We've gone through the experience of John Buchanan, who is very much a "**think outside the box**" sort of coach', said the 36-year-old leg-spinner.

The Guardian

The inability of governments to **think outside departmental boxes** bedevilled Mr Rae.

G&M National

Kids' bedrooms: Don't restrict yourself to pink or blue colour schemes – **think outside** with animal prints, wooden furniture and citrus colour.

The Herald

The two congressmen say they're **thinking outside the box**. Some critics of the idea, which has also been floated by Iranian exile groups, think they're just out of their minds.

Newsweek

tick all the boxes

If someone or something **ticks all the boxes**, they fulfil all the requirements for a specific role or purpose. It originates from the idea of an assessment form with a box for each criterion: if the person of thing you are assessing is ideal, you will put a tick in every box.

> Kizingo **ticks all the boxes** for a holiday hideaway: there are only seven bandas (simple palm-thatched cottages with walls of woven Pandanus), set in dunes just yards from the sea.
>
> *Daily Telegraph*

> All too often we think we've come up with the perfect name, one that **ticks all the boxes**. It's classy, quite cool and unusual – but without sounding contrived. Then you start mixing in baby circles and slowly it becomes clear that you're not the only one who had that particular brainwave.
>
> *BBC Magazine*

> But Strachan is desperate for a young, highly-rated left-back and he **ticks all the boxes**.
>
> *Daily Record*

> I met a new guy via an internet dating site. He **ticked all the boxes**, great sense of humour, he had a job, he didn't have two heads.
>
> *www.ivillage.co.uk*

touch base

To **touch base** with someone is to make personal contact with them. Originally an Americanism, this cliché has also established itself in British English.

Bono also **touched base** with the Scot to discuss progress when playing Glasgow last month. However, behind the famous interface with the public, 500 member groups have been working on strategies and policies.

The Herald

NASA astronaut Commander James Wetherbee will be dropping in on Cathays High School and Radyr Comprehensive School on Thursday March 2 to **touch base** with two youngsters who visited Kennedy Space Centre and Johnson Space Centre in America last year.

News Wales

'We will **touch base** in January and hopefully we can sit down again', said Sidwell, who joined Reading in 2003 from Arsenal. 'I want to stay in the Premier League for the rest of my career'.

Daily Mirror

'I plan to **touch base** with them throughout the year and if they are playing well during the Super 14 season they will certainly come into consideration'.

Rugby World

Don't worry, you're amongst friends now. Or perhaps you just wanted to **touch base** with the outside world, to check with the BBC whether anything important had happened.

BBC Magazine

when all is said and done

This is another cliché that introduces a summing-up of the subject under discussion. Like **at the end of the day**, it can be omitted without any loss of meaning.

> **When all is said and done** his biggest accomplishment was de-Sovietizing Russia, creating a free media, pluralism and electoral democracy. But surely Yeltsin's mistakes were greater than merely picking the wrong successor.
> *Newsweek International*

> All of us take pride and pleasure in the fact that we are unique, but I'm afraid that **when all is said and done** the police are right: it all comes down to fingerprints.
> David Sedaris *Santaland Diaries*

> Yesterday Murray hinted that the pressure from without was already greater than he liked it to be. It will not get any less, but **when all is said and done**, the real pressure will come from his opponents.
> *The Guardian*

> And the average price of new homes rose. **When all is said and done**, the forces sustaining growth seem to be outweighing those acting as brakes on the economy.
> *The Times*

> 'Justin is very honest and forthcoming and will continue to be, and **when all is said and done**, people will recognize that'.
> *The News & Observer*

abuse *and* **misuse**

If you **abuse** drugs, you take them illegally. If you **abuse** a person, you take undue advantage of them, misrepresent them, swear at them, maltreat them, or violate them sexually. The noun **abuse** refers to the act of doing any of the above. If you **misuse** something, you use it for the wrong purpose or in a wrong way. The noun **misuse** refers to improper use or use for a bad purpose.

It is estimated 344,000 people **abuse** cocaine in the UK every month.

BBC News

Nearly 80 per cent of A&E nurses have been **abused** at work in the past year.

Daily Mirror

Bali takes a hard line on drug **abuse** and it is not unusual for heroin dealers to face a firing squad.

Daily Record

Any time we get a report of child **abuse**, we have emergency response workers go out and investigate the report.

Los Angeles Times

The Federal Court found that a number of executives had **misused** their market power by engaging in exclusive deals to prevent parallel imports of CDs.

Sydney Morning Herald

Contractors will have to confront tales of **misuse** of federal funds, from Iraq to New Orleans.

The Times

accord *and* account

If you do something **of your own accord**, you do it
voluntarily and spontaneously. If you do something **on your
own account**, you do it for your own sake or on your own
behalf, not someone else's. The two are often confused.

> Sir John has no power to act **on his own accord** and must rely
> on the Cabinet Office for his investigatory staff.
>
> *Daily Telegraph*

Be careful when you use these phrases.

> Yet Abbey denied she was sent home in shame. She insisted
> she left **of her own accord** to protect her fella.
>
> *The Sun*

> His hands had curled into fists **of their own accord**; he forced
> himself to open them.
>
> C S FRIEDMAN *Crown of Shadows*

> But there's a fair bit the councils could be doing **on their own
> account** to make their finances more sustainable.
>
> *Sydney Morning Herald*

> I am curious **on my own account**, up to a point, but I've seen
> for myself what obsession has made of Azazir.
>
> JULIET E McKENNA *Eastern Tide*

adherence *and* adhesion

These words have similar meanings but they should be used differently. **Adherence** means sticking to your beliefs or remaining constant or loyal to a leader or party. **Adhesion** means a physical attachment or sticking between objects. They are sometimes confused.

> Texturing provided a strong adherence between the surface of a cell and the surface of a disk.
>
> *Science Daily*

> It may take natural disasters or a real fundamental crisis to break their adhesions to their traditional way of doing things.
>
> *The Industry Standard*

You should use **adherence** for the figurative sense of sticking and **adhesion** for the literal sense.

> A civilised society is judged by its **adherence** to the rule of law, to due process and the ease with which all people would have access to the law.
>
> *Sydney Morning Herald*

> Masters was an odd man out in an institution which demanded **adherence** to a strict moral and social code.
>
> *The Herald*

> Crushed leaves become slippery when wet, and the poor **adhesion** between wheel and track makes it difficult for trains to slow down and stop.
>
> *Physics Web*

> He started studying the **adhesion** of blood cells to the vascular wall, the inner lining of the blood vessels.
>
> *Science Daily*

adverse *and* averse

Adverse means contrary, opposed or unfavourable. **Averse** means disinclined, unwilling or reluctant. They are often confused.

> He enjoys fresh spring grass, although he's not adverse to a bit of late season hay when the grass is poor.
>
> *Washington Times*

> But the first real indication that the scandal has had an averse effect would come at an IOC Executive Board meeting in late June.
>
> *Newsweek*

Remember that **adverse** (opposed) is related to 'adversary' (an opponent), and **averse** (reluctant) is related to 'aversion' (reluctance).

> There is anecdotal evidence to suggest that the restructuring is having an **adverse** effect on recruitment.
>
> *The Herald*

> The State Department was forced into a policy U-turn after weeks of **adverse** publicity.
>
> *Daily Telegraph*

> The younger generation is most **averse** to saving with 28% of those aged between 16 and 24 choosing not to have a savings account.
>
> *The Guardian*

> I know that women are much more risk **averse** than men.
>
> *Daily Mail*

affect *and* effect

These words are close in meaning and are therefore often confused. The verb **affect** has two core meanings. If something **affects** you, it acts upon or influences you. If you **affect** a feeling or attitude, you make a show or pretence of having it. The noun **affect** is rare and its use is restricted to the context of psychology. **Effect**, on the other hand, can be a noun or a verb. The noun **effect** refers to the result of an action, the impression produced, or the meaning conveyed. If you **effect** something, you produce it or bring it about.

'I had the best job in the world, and if I had carried on it would have **affected** my ability to do that job at Wigan', he said.

Daily Telegraph

He says Australia stands out as one of the countries whose vegetation may be most **affected** by climate change.

Sydney Morning Herald

He was Southern, although after a few drinks he **affected** an alarming English drawl.

RUPERT EVERETT *Red Carpets and Other Banana Skins*

The weather was having a profound **effect** on my mood.
EWAN McGREGOR AND CHARLEY BOORMAN *Long Way Round*

Yet the overall **effect** was one of striking harmony, as every star-tile had a coppery ground of red, while the crosswise ones glowed gold.

JULIET E McKENNA *Eastern Tide*

But some changes can be **effected** without legislation.

The Times

alias *and* alibi

If you have an **alias**, you use a name other than your own original name, sometimes in order to cheat or defraud.
If you have an **alibi** for a crime, you claim that you were somewhere else when the crime was committed. The use of **alibi** to mean 'an excuse for failure' is informal. You should avoid using it in writing as many people consider it to be incorrect.

> When arrested last year by Irish police, Russell was living and working in Dublin under the **alias** David Carroll.
>
> *Seattle Times*

> Although he went by several **aliases**, he was identified as Dia Abdul Zahra Kadim, 37, from Hillah, south of Baghdad.
>
> *Philadelphia Online*

> He said he was instructed by Hunt in 1974 to back up an **alibi** for his whereabouts on the day Kennedy died, 11 years earlier.
>
> *Los Angeles Times*

> He sent texts to strengthen his **alibi** even though he knew his wife Jaspal was already dead, it was alleged.
>
> *The Sun*

> 'Mr Beattie, there are no **alibis** for your failure in health', Mr Howard told the audience.
>
> *Sydney Morning Herald*

> The archbishop warned, however, that this must not become an '**alibi**' for avoiding the issue.
>
> *The Herald*

allude *and* elude

If you **allude** to something, you refer to it indirectly or without mentioning it explicitly. If you **elude** someone, you escape from them in a clever or cunning way. If something you want **eludes** you, you cannot obtain it.

> The football association here had been **eluding** to the fact they'd appoint a local coach, so people felt let down.
>
> *The Herald*

> He was a fugitive long before the FBI put him on the most wanted list. How he managed to **allude** capture for so long is unclear at this point.
>
> *Spoken corpus*

When used correctly, **allude** always appears with the preposition 'to', while **elude** takes a direct object.

> This is made clear in the diary itself when the author **alludes** to several trips abroad as a roving reporter.
>
> PHILIP BOEHM (TRANSLATOR) *A Woman in Berlin*

> Rather, it is the Supreme Court's interpretation of the very Constitution to which Will **alludes**.
>
> *National Review Online*

> Trackers briefly caught sight of a brown bear blamed for killing livestock in southern Germany and Austria, but the animal **eluded** capture today by slipping into the dark.
>
> *Seattle Times*

> Ricky Ponting is confident the Australians are now ready for a tilt at the only major silverware to **elude** them – the Champions Trophy.
>
> *Sydney Morning Herald*

allusion, delusion *and* illusion

An **allusion** to someone or something is an indirect reference to it. A **delusion** is a false belief or the state of being deceived. An **illusion** is a deceptive appearance or a false impression of reality. The three are often confused.

> My parents made sure that I was under no **allusions** that I could and can go to war any time.
>
> *Spoken corpus*

> 'It's no optical **delusion**. It's closer tonight. I swear. Look, you can see a halo just like an angel 's'.
>
> *Pan MacMillan*

> At the beginning of this show he was talking, you know, making **illusions** to rape victims and their dress.
>
> *Spoken corpus*

As the above examples show, many of the mistakes around there three words occur in speech.

> In the earliest Buddhist scriptures there is an **allusion** to a story of human evolution, which is recounted in many of the subsequent Abhidharma texts.
>
> THE DALAI LAMA *The Universe in a Single Atom*

> I'm not under any **delusions** of perfection and I don't feel glamorous at all.
>
> *Daily Record*

> Renaissance artists used perspective to create the **illusion** of depth in a painting.
>
> *The Guardian*

ambiguous *and* ambivalent

If something is **ambiguous**, it is uncertain or can have more than one possible meaning. If a person is **ambiguous**, it means that they are hard to define or understand. If you are **ambivalent** about something, you have conflicting feelings about it at the same time.

> This meant that his position was highly **ambivalent**; he was appointed by the states, but had the right to appoint officials, often including the members of the states themselves.
>
> Bruce P Lenman *Dictionary of World History*

> 'Are you hungry for fame?' 'No; I feel very **ambiguous** about it'.
>
> *The Guardian*

You use **ambiguous** to describe a thing, situation, or someone other than yourself. You use **ambivalent** of people, either yourself or someone else.

> His **ambiguous** answer put a question mark over the U.N.'s stance on the death penalty.
>
> *Philadelphia Online*

> Billy Chenwith, Brenda's manic depressive brother in Six Feet Under, is an equally **ambiguous** character.
>
> *The Guardian*

> Even in my old age, I remain **ambivalent** about dogs.
>
> *Slate*

> Helen Mirren was **ambivalent** about becoming a dame. She never refers to herself as such.
>
> *BBC Magazine*

amend *and* emend

If a law or rule is **amended**, some of its details are altered with a view to improving it. If you **amend** a plan, a document, or the way you do something, you correct or improve it. If you **emend** something written, you make alterations to it in order to improve it. The verb **emend** should be used only of written text, while **amend** can be used of anything, including text.

> In addition we are looking to **amend** section three of the Computer Misuse Act to clarify that all means of interference to a computer system are criminalised.
>
> *Computing UK*

> It is cheaper for developers to pay the maximum on-the-spot fine of $600 than to **amend** building plans and lodge a new application.
>
> *Sydney Morning Herald*

> And if this new spirit of strict accuracy catches on, we fear Jack McConnell may be forced to **amend** his latest prize slogan.
>
> *Daily Record*

> Britain's biggest travel company called the judgment a 'watershed' and said it would **amend** the way it sells holidays accordingly.
>
> *Daily Telegraph*

> I also enjoyed VIVA CASTRO, later **emended** to VIVA CASTROL – who was the petrol freak?
>
> SALLY BEAUMAN *The Landscape of Love*

amiable *and* amicable

A person who is **amiable** has a sweet and friendly nature. An agreement or arrangement that is **amicable** is made or done in a friendly way.

> He struck up an amiable relationship with Margaret Thatcher whom he presented with a Georgian silver teapot at their first meeting.
>
> *The Times*

> 'I'm happy to talk to you, as long as it's not about me and Shaun Berrigan', said the **amicable** 22-year-old.
>
> *Sydney Morning Herald*

Remember that you use **amiable** to describe a person, and **amicable** to describe a deal or an agreement.

> Zac was an **amiable** enough companion. That was one of the problems. He was too **amiable**, too happy to go along with anything Tom suggested.
>
> WILLIAM C DIETZ *Enemy Within*

> The normally **amiable** Wenger was clearly agitated when asked about Cole after his team had beaten Schwadorf 8-1.
>
> *The Guardian*

> They are separating after nearly four years of marriage, blaming intrusion from the media and insisting their split is **amicable.**
>
> *Seattle Times*

> I had hoped they could find an **amicable** settlement but that doesn't seem to have happened.
>
> *Daily Mirror*

appraise *and* apprise

If you **appraise** something, you estimate its worth or set a price for it. If you **appraise** a person, you look closely at them or their work, in order to make a judgment about them. If you **apprise** someone of something, you inform them of it.

> I thought it appropriate that you are fully appraised of the expectations facing you this season.
>
> *Sydney Morning Herald*

> The tall woman in leathers eyed Kathryn up and down, apprising her as a threat.
>
> JAMES CLEMENS *Shadowfall*

Of the two words, **appraise** is the commoner, with **apprise** used mainly in formal contexts.

> This time, however, the ring **appraised** by the jeweller has been switched and he is now offered a fake in the hope that he will not bother to examine it a second time.
>
> JAMES MORTON AND GERRY PARKER *Gangland Bosses*

> She paused, **appraising** Isabel with piercing blue eyes. 'I lost my husband some years ago. He was an engineer too'.
>
> ALEXANDER MCCALL SMITH *Friends, Lovers, Chocolate*

> The younger brother of the Chief Minister said the party has sought time with the President to **apprise** him of the whole situation.
>
> *Times of India*

> It didn't take the widely reported UNICEF report to **apprise** us of that: it is common knowledge to almost anyone who has ventured into a city centre on a Saturday night.
>
> *The Guardian*

assure, ensure *and* insure

If you **assure** someone of something, you tell them it with confidence and without doubt. If success in a venture is **assured**, it is certain to happen. If you **ensure** that something happens, you make sure that it happens. If you **insure** a possession, you arrange for a sum of money to be paid to you if that possession is lost or damaged.

> An early start on withdrawal was needed to **assure** Iraqis that the British had no intention of staying permanently.
>
> *Sydney Morning Herald*

> O'Sullivan rounded off with a break of 90 in the penultimate frame then punched the air, waving at his fans once victory was **assured**.
>
> *The Sun*

> We can also combat dependency by **ensuring** that women and men have equal inheritance rights. In many hard-hit countries, women and orphans have none.
>
> *Newsweek*

> The glass-walled staircase is **insured** for £500,000.
>
> *Daily Telegraph*

Each of these words is derived from French *seur*, meaning 'sure', which itself comes from Latin *securus*, meaning 'safe'.

aural *and* oral

Something that is **aural** is received by or related to the ear.
Something that is **oral** is spoken by or related to the mouth.
The two are sometimes confused, although **oral** occurs far
more frequently than **aural**.

Both words are from Latin: **aural** from *auris*, meaning 'ear',
and **oral** from *os*, meaning 'mouth'.

> What we know for certain is that by the age of 20 weeks
> unborn children can respond to external **aural** stimuli, such as
> music and conversation.
>
> *Daily Telegraph*

> Some time around the start of the second hour of this **aural**
> water torture, it begins to look like a cunning plan by the
> woman we are waiting for.
>
> *The Herald*

> During pregnancy, **oral** medicines are not recommended and
> are usually replaced by insulin.
>
> *www.netdoctor.co.uk*

> She began collecting the **oral** histories of plural wives to
> publish in a book and created a website for her organisation,
> Principle Voices.
>
> *The Times*

avenge *and* revenge

If you **avenge** a person or a thing, you take vengeance for that person or for that thing. Although it is now quite common to read or hear **avenge oneself**, some people believe that use is incorrect so it is better to avoid it in writing. If you **revenge** something, you take vengeance for it. It is acceptable to write **revenge oneself**. The noun **revenge** means a malicious injury inflicted for an injury received. It is often used in sports to mean the opportunity of retaliation in a return match.

Then there is Grendel's mother, even fiercer and more monstrous, a swamp creature from hell bent on **avenging** her son.

Sydney Morning Herald

The Pashtunwali code of honour that extends a hand of hospitality to strangers in Afghanistan also has a flipside that dictates that a dishonour is **avenged.**

The Herald

In the tape, he vows to **revenge** the death of Abu Musab al-Zarqawi.

Slate

He had lost the desire to **revenge himself** on his aunts and uncle.

KATE ELLIOTT *Spirit Gate*

Finally she would have the **revenge** on Rama and his brother for which she had waited fourteen long years.

ASHOK BANKER *King of Ayodhya*

As Waddell danced with his players on the pitch, Killie tasted sweet **revenge** for Hearts ' 1-0 victory in the League Cup final of 1962.

The Herald

avert, avoid *and* evade

If you **avert** something bad, you stop it happening. If you **avoid** a person, you escape from having to see or speak to them. If you **avoid** a situation or event, you manage not to go to it or experience it. If you **evade** something, you escape it using cunning.

> What is the capacity of international institutions such as the UN to act to **avert** humanitarian crises?
>
> *Sydney Morning Herald*

> We often had a coffee and even went to Weight Watchers together. Now I'm **avoiding** her and I know she is puzzled, as well as hurt.
>
> *Daily Record*

> Pinochet **avoided** prosecution for years after his presidency.
>
> *Philadelphia Online*

> Most of those charged are accused of helping suspects to **evade** arrest or withholding information from police.
>
> *BBC News*

When it comes to taxes, there is a significant difference between **avoiding** tax, and **evading** tax.

> Tax evasion is illegal and the CBI will have nothing to do with such criminal behaviour. But tax **avoidance** – arranging one's affairs within existing legislation – is perfectly legitimate.
>
> *The Herald*

bail *and* bale

The noun **bail** has a number of meanings, including the money given to secure the release of an accused person, and the crosspiece on top of the stumps in a cricket wicket. The verb **bail** means to set someone free by paying a security for them, and to clear water out of a boat with a bucket. If you **bail out**, you clear water out of a boat using a bucket, you escape from an aeroplane by parachute, or you extricate yourself from a potentially difficult situation. The noun **bale** is a bundle or package of goods. The verb **bale** means to make into bundles or packages. You can use **bale out** as a variant of **bail out**. The various meanings of **bail** and **bale**, and the interchangeability of **bail out** and **bale out** mean that these words are often confused.

A court in Barbados returned his passport after increasing his **bail** from £5000 to £25,000.

Daily Mirror

Hair and Doctrove then lifted the **bails** and announced Pakistan's forfeiture, thereby handing victory to England.

Sydney Morning Herald

One of our cameramen got too close to the police vans and was himself arrested; he was **bailed** in the early hours.

JEREMY ISAACS *Look Me in the Eye*

I **bailed** faster and faster. My arms felt like they were about to fall out of their sockets.

SABINE KUEGLER *Jungle Child*

Inside the barn were **bales** of straw and bundles of green oats used for fodder for feeding the animals in winter.

FLAHPOINT

bated *and* baited

The phrase that means 'holding one's breath in fear or suspense' is **with bated breath**. **Bated** is the past tense and participle of the verb **bate**, meaning 'to abate, lessen or diminish'. **Baited** is the past tense and participle of the verb **bait**, which has various meanings, including 'to set a trap with food', 'to tempt', 'to set dogs upon' and 'to persecute or harass'. Many people confuse the two and incorrectly write 'with baited breath'.

> Every month in Zimbabwe, he would wait with **baited** breath for the latest golf magazine to arrive.
>
> *Daily Telegraph*

> The Sydney Conservatorium lecturer now waits with **baited** breath for his lucky find to arrive safely.
>
> *BBC Music*

If you think of **bated** as a shortened form of **abated**, it might be easier to remember that the correct spelling is **with bated breath**.

> We're waiting **with bated breath** to see if anything has changed.
>
> *Times of India*

> As Neil Armstrong became the first man to walk on the Moon in 1969, a global audience of 500 million people on Earth watched and listened **with bated breath.**
>
> *The Times*

biannual *and* biennial

An event that is **biannual** happens twice a year. An event that is **biennial** happens every two years, or lasts for two years. Understandably, these words are often confused.

> Woods is a member of the U.S. team for the Ryder Cup on Sept. 22-24 in Ireland. That's the biannual match-up between the best players in the U.S. and Europe.
>
> *Seattle Post–Intelligencer*

One way to differentiate between the two words is to think that if **annual** means 'once a year', **biannual** is two times as much, so means 'twice a year'.

> Bilimoria will co-chair the IBP's first **biannual** meeting of 2007.
>
> *Times of India*

> Meanwhile, in August 2006, South Australia member of parliament Ann Bressington proposed mandatory **biannual** drug testing of all the state's school students over the age of 14.
>
> *New Scientist*

> The chain has also signed a new six-year deal to be the key sponsor of the **biennial** Red Nose Day and Sport Relief campaigns.
>
> *The Herald*

> Beware all ye southerners, the Highlanders are gathering in preparation for their **biennial** march south with hope in their hearts and the Calcutta Cup in their possession.
>
> *Daily Telegraph*

bravado *and* bravura

Bravado is a display of bravery or boastful threatening.
Bravura is a brilliant or daring display. Something **bravura**
is performed with brilliance and daring. The two are
sometimes confused.

> There's an exhilarating sense of rhythm and a good deal
> of daring; a POV shot from a severed head one of several
> **bravado** moments.
>
> *Total Film*

Bravura is both a noun and an adjective; **bravado** is a noun.

> I thought I was a tough man, full of **bravado**, but I was
> shocked by what I saw.
>
> *Daily Mirror*

> Ballesteros played with imagination, **bravado** and a kind of
> operatic grandeur.
>
> *The Guardian*

> The **bravura** and individualism of his ink paintings of flowers,
> birds, fish and landscapes appealed to the Japanese.
>
> *Chambers Biographical Dictionary*

> Tipped for an Oscar, Hoffman brings all his talents to bear in
> a **bravura** performance as the flamboyant literary star.
>
> *The Guardian*

breach *and* breech

The noun **breach** is a break or act of breaking, either physical or figurative. If you **breach** something you make an opening in it. The **breech** is the lower back part of the body, and a **breech delivery** or **breech birth** is one in which the buttocks, and sometimes also the feet, come first. They are sometimes confused.

> Mr Mote will tell the inquiry that holding the funds **breeches** European Union (EU) rules.
>
> *Daily Telegraph*

> I'd had her by caesarean because she was **breach**, so I couldn't even cry. It was too painful.
>
> *The Sun*

One way to differentiate between these two is to associate **breach** with its meaning 'break', and note that they share the 'ea' spelling.

> She hunkered down lower as they came to the **breach** in the wall.
>
> JAMES CLEMENS *Shadowfall*

> Chertoff maintained he did not realize that New Orleans' levees had been **breached** until the next day.
>
> *Seattle Times*

> The prosecutor, Colonel Morris Davis, said the defence lawyer may have **breached** military law.
>
> *The Economist*

> Complications such as **breech birth** and infection were partly to blame for this increased risk, says Smith.
>
> *New Scientist*

brunt *and* butt

The **brunt** of a blow is the main force of it, so by extension the **brunt** of anything is its main shock or crisis. A **butt** is someone who is made the object of ridicule.

Over his years with Kathryn, he had been the **brunt** of her clever tongue and sharp wit.

James Clemens Shadowfall

Hans Christian Andersen's ugly duckling bears the **butt** of jokes from North London pond life in this contemporary retelling.

Times Online

A person can **carry** or **bear the brunt** of something, but they cannot *be* the **brunt**. A **brunt** is a thing and a **butt** is a person.

This is one tough chunk of land, taking the full **brunt** of winter storms that blow in from the Pacific.

Seattle Times

Crops such as stone fruit and grapes will be particularly vulnerable. Outback towns are already feeling the **brunt** of these changes.

Sydney Morning Herald

His sister, six years his junior, **bore the brunt** of their troubled home life and died of a heroin overdose in 1976.

The Guardian

She becomes the **butt** of jokes by the bitchy girls at the office and her only friend is Christina.

The Sun

When Derry crashed out of the Ulster Championship to Donegal, manager Crozier found himself the **butt** of criticism.

Belfast Telegraph

canvas *and* canvass

The noun **canvas** refers to a coarse cloth made of cotton or hemp, used for sails, tents, and for painting on. If you **canvass** or **canvass for** votes or contributions, you attempt to get them from people. To **canvass** also means to go from person to person seeking information. The noun **canvass** is a close examination or the act of seeking votes or information.

> He must have been knocked to the **canvass** about a dozen times.
>
> *BBC Magazine*

> Significantly the pollsters failed to **canvas** opinions in Saudi Arabia, Pakistan, Iraq or Iran.
>
> *Daily Telegraph*

If you associate **canvass** with an attempt to amass votes or information, you may find it easier to remember it has a double 's'.

> Upstairs, he fetched two long **canvas** bags from the closet and packed some clothes.
>
> NICHOLAS EVANS *The Loop*

> Now Italy's parties are **canvassing** for votes here.
>
> *Sydney Morning Herald*

> Although the report focused on academic achievements and the impact of the social mix, it also **canvassed** the views of pupils, parents and teachers.
>
> *The Guardian*

> And the **canvass** of the area for witnesses turned up nothing so far.
>
> *Daily Mirror*

censor, censure *and* censer

If you **censor** a book, letter, paper or film, you delete material that you consider to be inappropriate or offensive. A **censor** is an official whose job is to examine books, letters, papers and films with powers to censor them. If you **censure** someone, you blame or condemn them. The noun **censure** means an unfavourable opinion or judgement. A **censer** is a ceremonial container in which incense is burned.

> Mohammed told the Guantanamo panel he had been tortured but his exact words were **censored** by the Pentagon for 'security reasons'.
>
> *Daily Record*

> Before it could be released, it took four months for **censors** to comb through the movie.
>
> *Washington Times*

> The commission previously **censured** Jorgensen in 1996 for incompetence.
>
> *Seattle Times*

> No one who has been responsible for this debacle should escape **censure**.
>
> *Sydney Morning Herald*

> Inside, white-robed Orthodox priests chanted prayers and swung **censers**.
>
> *Jerusalem Post*

ceremonial *and* ceremonious

The adjective **ceremonial** means 'relating to or of the nature of a ceremony'. **Ceremonious** means 'scrupulously careful about observing formalities'. The two are sometimes confused.

> Between then and the end of July, there were attacks on counter-revolutionaries in eight other localities across the country, including the **ceremonious** killing of two priests in Bordeaux on the 14th.
>
> DAVID ANDRESS *The Terror*

> It features not only **ceremonious**, sacrificial oxen but a humble onion, goat's cheese grated with a bronze grater, and lentils.
>
> *Times Literary Supplement*

Ceremonial is by far the commoner of the two adjectives.

> A 200-strong military honour guard, wearing full **ceremonial** dress and black armbands formed on the tarmac to escort his casket from the plane to a private ceremony.
>
> *Sydney Morning Herald*

> He joined up at 17 and carried out **ceremonial** duties in November 2004 at the funeral of Princess Alice, Duchess of Gloucester.
>
> *The Sun*

> 'I like changing for dinner', I said. 'At least, I should like it if I ever had occasion to ... I'd like to make a long **ceremonious** toilette every night and appear looking fancy as the Pope'.
>
> ROSAMOND LEHMANN *The Weather in the Streets*

childish *and* childlike

Someone or something that is **childish** is like a child,
especially in a silly or annoying way. Someone or something
that is **childlike** is like a child, especially in an innocent
or sweet way. **Childish** is always used disapprovingly.
Childlike does not carry the same negative connotations as
childish.

> A treasure hunt in the gardens had been arranged later in the
> afternoon for those children who didn't think such **childish**
> pursuits beneath them.
>
> IAIN BANKS *The Steep Approach to Garbadale*

> Dina experienced another volcanic spurt of anger. **Childish**
> and petty it might be, but it was also deeply satisfying. Archie
> was asking for it.
>
> DEBORAH WRIGHT *Love Eternally*

> It became so bad in France on Sunday that Renault actually
> issued a **childish** tit-for-tat press release while the race was
> taking place.
>
> *The Guardian*

> He ordered two teas with a **childlike** enthusiasm and lit
> another cigarette with a gold-plated lighter.
>
> COURTTIA NEWLAND *The Dying Wish*

> This was why I was unable to enter into that **childlike**
> innocence without which no novel is possible.
>
> *The Guardian*

> He had a curious **childlike** devotion to his two frightful
> brothers.
>
> SUSAN HOWATCH *The Rich are Different*

classic *and* classical

These adjectives share a number of meanings so it is unsurprising that they are often confused. However, there are also contexts in which it is preferable to use one and not the other. The meanings of **classic** include 'of the highest class or rank, especially in literature or art', 'chaste, refined and restrained', 'traditionally accepted, long or well established', and 'excellent or definitive'. The meanings of **classical** include 'of orchestral or chamber music, as opposed to jazz, folk or music' and 'relating to Greek and Latin studies'.

This is the **classic** novel of English working life.

BBC Magazine

The 39-year-old singer has **classic** beauty.

Sydney Morning Herald

There are the usual **classic** dishes on offer such as korma, dansak, bhuna.

Daily Record

Anne Bancroft turned in a **classic** performance with her portrayal of the predatory older woman.

Daily Mail

She now works for a management company specialising in **classical** musicians.

Sydney Morning Herald

Our schools offer traditional subjects such as Latin, Greek and **classical** studies.

The Herald

climatic *and* climactic

The adjective **climatic** means 'of or relating to the climate of a place'. The adjective **climactic** means 'of or relating to a climax'. The similarity of their spelling sometimes leads to confusion.

> Mystery Jets brought the ShockWaves NME Awards Tour 2006 to a **climatic** close in London last night.
>
> *NME*

> The finding is significant for understanding what can happen to ecosystems when confronted with the interrelated **climatic** and atmospheric changes that are observed today.
>
> *Science Daily*

It is helpful to remember that **climatic** is derived from **climate,** and the first 6 letters of these words are identical.

> We tried to do the lift (the **climactic** dance bit when Johnny holds Baby over his head) in our local swimming pool.
>
> *Daily Mail*

> At the **climactic** moment in the ceremony, Napoleon took the crown from the altar and placed it on his own head.
>
> *The Herald*

> Mounting scientific evidence now suggests that large changes in **climatic** conditions have occurred across the globe over the last millennium.
>
> *Science Daily*

> We have five different **climatic** zones from desert to snowy peaks over 4000 metres high.
>
> *Sydney Morning Herald*

coherence *and* cohesion

Both **coherence** and **cohesion** are derived from the verb **cohere**, meaning 'to stick together', 'to be consistent' and 'to fit together in an orderly whole', but each is used in a slightly different way. **Coherence** is consistency or a tendency to cohere. **Cohesion** is the act of sticking together. Given their close connection, it is not surprising that the two are often confused. A rule to help distinguish between them is that, generally, **coherence** is used of ideas, plans and writing, while **cohesion** is used of groups of people.

The government's approach lacks **coherence**. A series of measures produced more or less hysterically over recent years does not amount to a strategy.

The Times

The accounts and insights inject a sense of drama and narrative **coherence** to a story that's mostly been told in news grabs.
Sydney Morning Herald

This is an outstanding example of how partnership working can contribute to a local economy, improve the physical environment and strengthen community pride and **cohesion.**
News Wales

Stirling's recovery was far from complete, his career as a driver was over and, without his leadership, the team lacked **cohesion**.

Daily Telegraph

comparable *and* comparative

The adjective **comparable** means 'able to be or worthy of being compared'. The adjective **comparative** means 'making or estimated by a comparison with something else'.

> The report says it has very high confidence that the last few decades of the 20th Century were warmer than any **comparable** period in the last 400 years.
>
> *BBC News*

> An expert examined the seized paintings and he said they weren't of very high quality - not **comparable** with the good forgeries made by Konrad Kujau.
>
> *The Times*

> In Israel, the status of gays and lesbians is more **comparable** with Western Europe.
>
> *www.sfgate.com*

> He doesn't seem a whit embarrassed by his **comparative** lack of height.
>
> Lauren Henderson *Exes Anonymous*

> Researchers looked at the **comparative** cost of more than 200 items.
>
> *Daily Telegraph*

> The children are taught Hebrew and Arabic and learn **comparative** religion.
>
> *Sydney Morning Herald*

complacent, complaisant *and* compliant

Someone who is **complacent** is self-satisfied and has insufficient regard for approaching problems and dangers. A **complaisant** person is willing to comply with the wishes of others in order to please them. Someone who is **compliant** is submissive and tends to yield to the wishes of others. The connotations of **compliant** are more negative than those of **complaisant**.

A new report from US security firm McAfee has suggested that Apple users are **complacent** about security.
Computing UK

I had even told her to take a lover because I had realized it was better to be a **complaisant** husband than a deserted one.
ALLAN MASSIE *Sins of the Fathers*

He is obviously unformed, a malleable and **compliant** young man who could be shaped and moulded into something formidable, distinguished even.
JUDITH GOULD *Dreamboat*

compliment *and* complement

A **compliment** is an expression of admiration or praise. If you **compliment** someone or something you express your admiration or praise for that person or thing. A **complement** is something that completes or fills another thing up, or the number or quantity required to make something complete. The verb complement means 'to be the complement of'.

> The class will also be **complimented** by a range of other popular cruiser racers such as veteran campaigner Peter Schofield's Zarafa.
>
> *Yachting and Boating World*

> Private Morris was particularly pleased when members of the Royal family **complemented** him on his turnout and appearance.
>
> *Daily Telegraph*

It is helpful to remember that **complement** is related to **complete**, and the first 6 letters of the words are identical.

> It's not a **compliment** for a woman to be told she looks like a man.
>
> *Newsweek*

> While **complimenting** the police on their contribution, he also calls for more work to be done in Abu Ghosh.
>
> *Jerusalem Post*

> The impossible beauty of the Parthenon was **complemented** by the panorama across the city.
>
> *Daily Telegraph*

> Small wonder, perhaps, that the average Scottish battalion is 70 soldiers short of its full **complement** of 650.
>
> *The Herald*

The adjective derived from **compliment** is **complimentary**, and the adjective from **complement** is **complementary**.

□ 128 □

comprehensible *and* comprehensive

Someone or something that is **comprehensible** is capable of being understood. Something that is **comprehensive** contains many things or everything. A person cannot be **comprehensive**.

'The light of my life disappeared', Amarhanov said in a rush of anguished words barely **comprehensible** beneath the sobs.
Philadelphia Online

Breton and Cornish were closely related and remained mutually **comprehensible** languages until the eighteenth century.

ROBERT WINDER *Bloody Foreigners*

Clarke says that a larger, more **comprehensive** study of the penguin family tree is necessary before the full story of early penguins in the Land of Fire can be told.
Science Daily

A **comprehensive** report, including recommendations about where to put John Marshall students, is due this fall.
Seattle Times

Both words are derived from **comprehend**, which itself comes from Latin *com*, meaning 'with' and *prehendere*, meaning 'to seize'.

continual *and* continuous

These are two of the most commonly confused words in English. Something that is **continual** happens or is done constantly, repeatedly or persistently. Something that is **continuous** happens without interruption.

> Johns has been troubled by **continual** problems with a knee injury that required surgery last month.
> *Sydney Morning Herald*

> As for Anthony, he admits he is happy to be the butt of Simon's **continual** comments that he is 'odd'.
> *The Sun*

> Soon after their marriage Stephanie became disenchanted with her husband and his **continual** infidelities caused her great pain.
> MADELEINE MASSON *Christine*

> There was no shortage of TV footage of the fiesta with two channels each offering 10 hours of **continuous** coverage of the Barca players' open-top bus tour round the city.
> *The Herald*

> The economy has enjoyed five years of **continuous** growth since then.
> *The Economist*

> On that Ashes tour a 40-over game was hastily arranged after three days of **continuous** rain caused the Test match to be abandoned.
> *The Guardian*

cord *and* chord

A **cord** is a small rope or a thick string. A **cord** is also a part of the body that resembles a cord, as in the **vocal cords**. A **chord** is a group of notes played simultaneously on a musical instrument. A **chord** is also a sensitive area of a person's feelings, as in **touch a chord**.

'Because of where she was we cut the umbilical chord and put the baby on Linda's tummy for a couple of minutes and then got her ready to go in the ambulance to hospital'.

News Wales

Sir Cliff appears to have touched a cord with his latest song, which alludes to the world's modern inventions including mobile phones, fax machines, satellites and microwaves.

Daily Telegraph

Do not confuse these two words.

The canvas roll had been tied shut with a slender **cord**; unknotting it, he set the string aside.

CS FRIEDMAN *Crown of Shadows*

Simon wanted a second opinion so we went to London's Harley Street where the doctor found a nodule on my left vocal **cord**.

The Sun

She arrived on the first day only able to play two **chords** and now she is phenomenal.

Daily Record

Warm-hearted, emotional and ultimately redemptive, the film struck an instant **chord** with Sundance audiences.

The Herald

council *and* counsel

A **council** is an assembly called together for advice, administration or legislation. The adjective **council** means 'relating to or provided by a council'. The noun **counsel** is advice or a person who gives advice, especially in a legal case. The verb **counsel** means 'to advise or to warn'. If you **counsel** someone with a problem, you help adjust to or deal with that problem.

> The Planning Minister now has the discretion to overrule local **councils** on development applications and hand decisions over to expert panels appointed by him.
>
> *Sydney Morning Herald*

> He said a shortage of **council** housing was pushing up prices, with just 25,000 homes built last year compared with 150,000 in 1996.
>
> *Daily Record*

> To the girl's alarm, instead of offering sympathy and wise **counsel**, the older woman burst into floods of anxious tears.
>
> *Mary S Lovell Bess of Hardwick*

> Paul Drum, senior tax **counsel** for the accounting group CPA Australia, said charitable donations to the family would be gifts, with no tax consequences.
>
> *Sydney Morning Herald*

> Mr Doherty's defence **counsel** said the singer was eligible for a licence, but had not applied for one after passing his driving test.
>
> *BBC Entertainment*

> And she revealed she had **counselled** victims who lost limbs in the 7/7 suicide bombings.
>
> *The Sun*

credible *and* creditable

Someone or something that is **credible** is capable of being believed. A **credible** person is also someone who seems worthy of belief or confidence. Something **creditable** brings credit or honour and deserves praise.

> But Silberstein, who remains a professor at Swinburne University's Brain Sciences Institute, is a creditable neuroscientist.
>
> *Sydney Morning Herald*

> 'We'd like to do better. But we think it's a pretty credible result from a tough world', he said.
>
> *Sydney Morning Herald*

Both people and things can be **credible**, but only things can be **creditable**.

> The most **credible** witness was Chris Gibson, who had 12 years' experience with the Royal Observer Corps and was an expert on recognising aircraft.
>
> *The Guardian*

> It astounds me that the Treasury does not have a comprehensive, **credible** plan for closing the tax gap.
>
> *Washington Times*

> Contrary to Lexington's expectations, Ms Pelosi has put in a **creditable** performance as opposition leader.
>
> *The Economist*

> Hadden guided his side to a **creditable** third place in the Six Nations Championship.
>
> *Rugby World*

defective *and* deficient

Something that is **defective** is faulty is some way. Something or someone that is **deficient** in something is lacking in that particular thing. They are sometimes confused.

> For a moment the France coach gives a passable impression of a steam engine with a **deficient** safety valve.
>
> *The Guardian*

> We fear it is certain that the grouse this year, both in Dumfriesshire and Galloway, are sadly **defective** in numbers.
>
> *The Herald*

A general rule is that **deficient** can be used of people and things, while **defective** should be for things only.

> Lisa and Ruth Bendle carried a **defective** gene which killed their father, grandmother and cousin.
>
> *The Sun*

> He's paying for a product that is **defective**, and the law is pretty clear that if someone sold you a defective product they have a duty to repair it.
>
> *Daily Telegraph*

> It seemed strange that someone whose taste in food was so highly developed could be completely **deficient** in any musical taste whatsoever.
>
> ANTHONY CAPELLA *The Food of Love*

> In the Philippines, where this study was conducted, as many as 60 percent of the women may be iron **deficient**.
>
> *Science Daily*

definite *and* definitive

Something that is **definite** is clearly defined or fixed. An event that is **definite** is certain to take place. If you are **definite** about something, you are sure that it is true or is certain to happen. Something that is **definitive** is the most authoritative, expert or complete of its kind.

There's a **definite** Norse influence here, after all the Shetlands are closer to Bergen than they are to Aberdeen, while London and Reykjavik are practically equidistant from Lerwick.
CHARLIE CONNELLY AND ALEX JENNINGS *Attention All Shipping*

Chief Executive Gary Kelly has said neither change is **definite**, and that Southwest won't eliminate what it calls 'open seating' until late next year, at the earliest.
Seattle Times

A forensic team is now on site investigating the cause. It's still too early to be **definite** about what the cause was.
Belfast Telegraph

So far, there is no **definitive** evidence on the connection between dopamine enhancers, known as agonists, and compulsive gambling.
Sydney Morning Herald

The first **definitive** set of rules governing Gaelic spelling, punctuation and grammar in almost a quarter of a century has been published.
The Herald

□ 135 □

defuse *and* diffuse

If you **defuse** a bomb, you remove its fuse in order to make it harmless. If you **defuse** a difficult situation, you remove the tension or danger from it. If you **diffuse** something, you cause it to be circulated or spread in all directions. The adjective **diffuse** means 'widely spread'.

> Both police and the politicians should be stopped from making divisive comments about ethnic communities, and instead take steps to diffuse racial tensions.
> *Sydney Morning Herald*

> Wyl's shock was evident and they both laughed in embarrassment which, surprisingly, helped to **diffuse** the awkwardness.
> Fiona McIntosh *Blood and Memory*

As the examples above show, confusing these two verbs can, at the very least, be misleading

> In March 2004 police **defused** a huge bomb less than five minutes before it was timed to explode outside the consulate.
> *Jerusalem Post*

> A showdown meeting with key investors earlier this week appears to have **defused** any major institutional rebellion.
> *The Herald*

> Gas does not behave like that: it **diffuses** in all directions.
> Clive Prince and Lynn Picknett *Turin Shroud*

> The NIE report indicates that America's success against Al Qaeda has led to the enemy becoming more **diffuse** and independent.
> *Los Angeles Times*

derisive *and* derisory

Someone who is **derisive** is scoffing or mocking. Something that is **derisory** is ridiculous or ridiculously inadequate.

If you wanted to be **derisive**, you could say the music was very safe, but you could also say it was accomplished and mature.

Seattle Times

In a screening this week in godless New York, there was **derisive** laughter in the cinema.

Sydney Morning Herald

I agree that the Narnia books are racist and misogynist. They also are **derisive** about vegetarianism and liberal education.

BBC Entertainment

The increase in tax on gas guzzlers is **derisory** and will hardly pay for the new paperwork.

The Guardian

A Welsh farm leader today attacked 'the **derisory** share of the milk price paid to the producer'.

New Wales

The armed forces are used to being ignored by the Ministry of Defence, most notably with regard to a **derisory** level of consultation on the imposition of the new Armed Forces Pension Scheme.

The Herald

detract *and* distract

To **detract** from something is to diminish it or reduce its importance. To **distract** someone is to draw their attention onto something else or in several other directions. The two are sometimes confused.

> Woods insisted that he would not let the episode **distract** from his enjoyment of Ireland.
>
> *Sydney Morning Herald*

> As if I would let anything detract me from the joy of the moment.
>
> ELAINE DUNDY *The Old Man and Me*

The verb **detract** is always followed by the preposition 'from'.

> In any case, Wilson's remarkable literary skills should not **detract** from his achievements as a scientist.
>
> *The Guardian*

> Aston Barrett and his brother literally created the sound of the Wailers, though this is not for a minute to **detract** from the extraordinary song-writing ability of Mr Marley.
>
> *Belfast Telegraph*

> Jim puts a sick bowl on his head to **distract** me from my contractions.
>
> *The Mirror*

> Female drivers are more likely to be **distracted** by stunning scenery than by a hunky man, a survey revealed yesterday.
>
> *Daily Record*

discreet *and* discrete

Someone who is **discreet** is careful in their actions and choice of words, and is able to keep secrets. **Discrete** means separate, distinct or consisting of individual parts. The two are often confused.

'Centacare's role would be small and **discrete**', he said.
Sydney Morning Herald

In this state, electrons as we know them decompose so that electric charge is no longer transported in **discreet** lumps of charge.
Physics Web

Discreet is used of people and their behaviour, and **discrete** is used of things.

We also love her because she's beautiful, **discreet** and is rarely ever seen partying with people named Hilton.
New York Post

If I ever took a different girl to the same place, the waiters were **discreet** and never mentioned it.
Daily Mirror

Grid computing works excellently for computation of large data sets that can be broken down into **discrete** tasks.
Science Daily

With film on TV you see 25 **discrete** images per second.
The Guardian

distinct *and* distinctive

Something that is **distinct** is separate, well-defined, or unmistakable. Something that is **distinctive** is easily recognizable or characteristic of its kind.

> The report identified six **distinct** groups of mobile phone users: Generation Mobile, Phonatics, Practical Parents, Fingers & Thumbs, Smart Connecteds and Silver Cynics.
>
> *Computing UK*

> I had the **distinct** impression that she had been going to say something else, but I didn't push.
>
> JIM BUTCHER *Grave Peril*

> He was calm and distanced enough to notice once again the **distinct** smell of leaf mould in the cold air.
>
> HANNAH MCDONALD *Julianna Kiss*

> In November 1941, he reported that all the Japanese ships in Kobe Harbour were painting out their **distinctive** markings with grey paint.
>
> *Sydney Morning Herald*

> Fox's **distinctive** New Zealand accent is as strong as the coffee she has ordered.
>
> *The Herald*

> The **distinctive** call of fiordland penguins has been described as a cross between a grunting pig and a goose with a cold.
>
> *Daily Mail*

drawback *and* downfall

A **drawback** is a disadvantage. The **downfall** of a person or thing is its ruin, failure or humiliation.

> I think everyone deserves a break at some stage. That's probably the only downfall going into Asia. It's going to be very hard for us.
>
> *Sydney Morning Herald*

The similarity between **downfall** and **downside** (a disadvantage) leads people to use **downfall** when they should use **drawback** instead.

> The only real **drawback** to skiing in Japan is the time it takes to get here.
>
> *Daily Telegraph*

> In the three years since the **downfall** of Saddam Hussein, Iraq has descended into bloody lawlessness.
>
> *The Guardian*

> The prime minister knows very well the part the poll tax played in Margaret Thatcher's **downfall.**
>
> *The Herald*

> The BBC blamed competition from 24-hour music channels and the internet for the **downfall** of Top of the Pops.
>
> *Daily Mail*

economic *and* economical

Although these two adjectives are closely related, each does tend to be used in its own particular contexts. **Economic** means 'relating to economics or the economy'. **Economic** also means 'capable of yielding a profit'. **Economical** means 'thrifty or not wasteful'. If someone is **economical with the truth**, they cause deception by revealing only a selection of available information.

> **Economic** growth has been slow by comparison with other countries in Latin America.
>
> *The Economist*

> More than any other entrepreneur of the sixties, Terence Conran personified the cultural and **economic** trends of the day.
>
> DOMINIC SANDBROOK *White Heat*

> He added that with the business losing money week by week it was not **economic** to continue trading.
>
> *The Herald*

> Environment groups are calling for government intervention to ensure the introduction of cleaner, more **economical** vehicles.
>
> *Sydney Morning Herald*

> But Nolan's film is admirably **economical** in its storytelling, and resists losing itself in its hero's process of transformation.
>
> *The Herald*

> The MoD has been consistently **economical with the truth** on this matter.
>
> *Daily Telegraph*

effective, effectual, efficient *and* efficacious

These adjectives have overlapping meanings and are often used as if they are interchangeable. However, each does have its own particular usage. Something **effective** is capable of producing the desired result or effect. Something that is **effectual** has successfully produced the desired result. Something or someone **efficient** is capable of doing what is required, while doing it in speedy and competent way. Something **efficacious** is capable of producing the result intended; it used in formal contexts, and almost always in relation to drugs and medical treatments.

> We welcome any advances in scientific research that may speed up the development of an **effective** treatment for cystic fibrosis, which affects millions across the world.
>
> *The Guardian*

> The 'long, national nightmare' to which Mr. Ford referred upon taking office really did need to come to an end. And he took the most decisive and **effectual** measure possible to end it.
>
> *Washington Times*

> Scotland, as indeed the rest of the UK, can boast of the largest average herd size in the European Union – and some of the most **efficient** producers.
>
> *The Herald*

> This new compound is highly **efficacious** at inhibiting tumour growth and works by acting on two separate mechanisms that are involved in the development and perpetuation of human cancer cells.
>
> *Science Daily*

equable *and* equitable

Something **equable** is uniform or unvarying. An **equable** person is even-tempered. Something that is **equitable** is fair or just. People sometimes use **equable** when **equitable** is meant.

> In truth, the insurgency brought about freedom or peace such as that which Tito, Ceausescu, Franco or Idi Amin would have suggested was **equable** and necessary for state control.
>
> *The Times*

The adjective **equitable** is not used of people. Of the two adjectives, **equitable** occurs far more commonly than **equable**.

> An **equable** temperature, he used to say, is the secret of a healthy, contented wine.
>
> Peter Mayle *A Good Year*

> Ambrose was an **equable**, patient and good-humoured man who never raised his voice in anger.
>
> *The Guardian*

> Ms Bachelet, who was jailed and tortured by Chile's former military junta, has promised to build a more **equitable** and tolerant society.
>
> *BBC World News*

> When a drought devastated southern Africa, the government organised an efficient and **equitable** distribution of grain and no one went hungry.
>
> *Sydney Morning Herald*

evoke *and* invoke

If something **evokes** a memory or a feeling, it brings it
on. If someone or something **evokes** a response, it causes
that response. If you **invoke** a god, you call upon him to
help you. If you **invoke** a law or procedure, you put it into
practice.

Songs from the bygone era and re-enactment of Churchill's
historic speeches **evoked** memories of wartime Britain.

The Herald

Newborn babies listen to music through headphones in a
hospital. It reportedly **evokes** well-being and harmony after
birth.

Daily Record

The researchers then played synthetic versions of the signature
whistles of other dolphins through underwater loudspeakers to
see if they would **evoke** a response in the captive animals.

The Times

This was before the Supreme Court ruled that it is
unconstitutional for anyone to **invoke** God's name for
anything at any time during a graduation ceremony, unless of
course somebody sneezes.

Newsweek

Dvorak Uncensored, the blog produced by PC Magazine
columnist John C Dvorak, chided Baskins for **invoking** her
Fifth Amendment rights during the hearing.

The Slate

exalt *and* exult

If you **exalt** someone, you place them in a high position of respect and praise them. If you **exult**, you are intensely joyful. People often confuse them.

> But he was not afraid. He was almost exalted. 'We attack at midnight', the general said.
> Cynthia Harrod-Eagles *The Burning Roses*

> Resistance to honouring a politician is something to which Brits can relate. The willingness to exult a sinner, rather than extol a saint or educationist, is more complex.
> *The Herald*

The verb **exalt** takes a direct object. The verb **exult** does not.

> In western accounts, Saladin was a model of chivalry and ranked in greatness alongside Greek heroes. He was also **exalted** by Sir Walter Scott.
> *The Herald*

> In the iconography of American history, no group or idea is more **exalted** than the United States Marine Corps.
> *Sydney Morning Herald*

> He knew he was a star and **exulted** in it.
> *Daily Mirror*

> In some strange way I even **exulted** that I had been branded with the same illness as Keats, Stevenson, Emily Brontë, Francis Thomson and DH Lawrence.
> *The Herald*

fatal *and* fateful

An accident, injury or illness that is **fatal** leads to a person's death. Something **fateful** is decisive or has significant consequences. Often something that is **fateful** can be **fatal** as well, but the two adjectives are not synonymous.

A serving police officer has been charged with road traffic offences after a **fatal** road traffic accident.

The Herald

Eating small amounts of dark chocolate every day can help protect against **fatal** blood clots, doctors have found.

Daily Record

There have been 18 **fatal** alligator attacks in Florida since 1948.

The Sun

When Katrina made that **fateful** eastward turn three days before slamming into New Orleans, most people weren't home listening to their radios for weather advisories.

Newsweek

The 73-year-old Hanson was describing the moment before he watched the plane become the second to hit the Twin Towers on that **fateful** day.

Seattle Times

faze and phase

If something or someone **fazes** you, it worries or perturbs you. The verb **phase** means 'to do in phases or stages'. The two words are homophones and, as a result, **phase** is often used where **faze** is meant. Consequently, people sometimes write **phased** instead of **fazed** and **unphased** instead of **unfazed**.

> As Ferguson said in his post-match assessment: 'He was marvellous, nothing **phases** him'.
>
> *The Sun*

> But Eriksson is not **phased** by the weight of public expectation, nor does he expect his players to buckle under it either.
>
> *Daily Record*

> A path for appassionati willing to muddy their feet and close their eyes, brave and **unphased**, as we speed past the Gucci outlet.
>
> MARLENA DE BLASI *A Thousand Days in Tuscany*

The words **faze** and **phase** are completely unrelated. **Faze** comes from Old English *fēsian*, meaning 'to drive away', while **phase** is derived from Greek *phaein*, meaning 'to shine'.

> When she was being grilled by the dragons she kept her composure and nothing seemed to **faze** her.
>
> *Daily Telegraph*

> Meanwhile, Freeman clearly isn't **fazed** by the idea of a fundamental restructuring of the trucking sector.
>
> *Los Angeles Times*

> But the market appeared to be **unfazed** by the Democratic sweep of both houses of Congress in this year's elections.
>
> *Sydney Morning Herald*

fewer *and* less

The confusion over the usage of **fewer** and **less** is widespread in English. The commonest mistake is to use **less** when it ought to be **fewer**.

The supermarket had erected a neat little aisle just for the 15 items or *less* customers.

Sydney Morning Herald

I'm not sure there are **less** people going into software testing, but there is greater demand for them as firms are finally focusing more on software quality.

Computing UK

When you are talking about people or things that can be counted (that is, count nouns), you should use **fewer**. When you are talking about an amount of something that cannot be counted (that is, uncount nouns), you should use **less**.

This would also result in 8,000 **fewer** cars on the road.

News Wales

How can you work more efficiently with **fewer** nurses?

Daily Telegraph

There are **fewer** houses on the market now.

Philadelphia Online

Patients of all ages in sunny rooms had **less** pain.

Belfast Telegraph

They ensure they include fresh fruit and vegetables, cook with **less** fat and consume **less** sugar.

The Herald

We can simply burn **less** oil by driving less and walking more.

Daily Mirror

fictional *and* fictitious

The meanings of these adjectives fall within the same broad semantic area – that of invention or untruth – but they have different usages. Something that is **fictional** is related to fiction, the branch of literature concerning story-telling. Something that is **fictitious** is false or made-up, especially in order to deceive.

Brown's real name is Royston Vasey, the name of the **fictional** town in TV comedy *The League of Gentlemen*.

Sydney Morning Herald

Ecclesiastical historian Vivian Green, who was an inspiration for John le Carre's **fictional** spymaster George Smiley, has died at the age of 89.

The Herald

A worker in a nuclear power plant near the **fictional** Middle America town of Springfield, his life is a series of mistakes and accidents.

Belfast Telegraph

She would create a cheque for a **fictitious** payee, log off and log on again using her supervisor's name and password, and authorise the payment.

RTE News Online

Sarabjit Singh and Gurpreet Singh were owners of **fictitious** companies. Their 'employees' had salary accounts with perfect paperwork.

Times of India

Yet here I am, an undercover journalist with a **fictitious** name, inside their East Midlands operation.

Daily Telegraph

flaunt *and* flout

If you **flaunt** something, you show it off or display it ostentatiously. If you **flout** an order or rule, you defy it deliberately. People often confuse these verbs.

> Dawn became the second person to leave the *Big Brother* house in 48 hours yesterday when Big Brother kicked her out for **flaunting** the house rules.
>
> *More Magazine*

If you struggle to remember which is which, try to associate **flaunt** with something other people 'want'. This rhyming words might help.

> It sickens me how they continue to **flaunt** their wealth, while donors wonder what happened to the money they thought they were giving to charity.
>
> *Daily Record*

> She was pictured on the beach in Dubai this week **flaunting** her new size 10 figure.
>
> *Daily Mail*

> Snack and fast food companies routinely **flout** guidelines on television advertising to children and are deliberately encouraging a junk food culture.
>
> *Sydney Morning Herald*

> The committee claimed that Microsoft has **flouted** sanctions that should have levelled the playing field for companies that make work group servers.
>
> *Computing UK*

flounder *and* founder

If you **flounder**, you struggle with violent or awkward movements. To **flounder** also means to stumble helplessly in thinking or speaking. If a project or plan **founders**, it fails. If a ship **founders**, it fills with water and sinks. People sometimes use **flounder** where **founder** ought to be used.

> Nations are scrambling to sign up free-trade partners as multi-country talks to liberalize international commerce **flounder**.
> *G&M National*

The verb **flounder** is used far less frequently than **founder**, so think carefully before you use it, in case it is really **founder** you mean.

> He lets me out instead in a kayak, which is great, apart from the bit where I have to **flounder** back to land while an attendant rescues my craft from Jamaica.
> *Guardian Travel*

> 'My mother ...' she says, and the word **flounders** in mid-air.
> *Guardian Books*

> A plan for a Europe-wide carbon tax had **foundered** in the early 1990s in the face of vehement opposition from industry.
> *London Review of Books*

> When two days had passed without word, he became convinced that the little sloop had **foundered** in the Channel.
> EMMA DONOGHUE *Life Mask*

good *and* well

There is often confusion over when to use **good** and when to use **well**. **Good** is an adjective. Although often heard in informal speech, **good** should not be used as an adverb. The adjective **well** means in good health. The adverb **well** means in a satisfactory, pleasing, skilful or correct manner. Although **well** is often heard in informal speech as an adverb modifying an adjective, this usage should be avoided in formal writing and speech, as many people consider it incorrect.

'They did play **good** the week before but on the night the other side was just too committed', McCarthy said.

Sydney Morning Herald

'I did it all on MySpace so I'm **well** happy about that'.

The Sun

It is acceptable to use **well** as an adverb to modify a past participle, such as 'a well-planned operation' or 'well-polished shoes' and 'the cloth looked well brushed' or 'she's been well fed'.

I think in the early games we have played we have had a **good** passing game, and we are creating lots of chances.

The Herald

He was not invited because he is not **well**.

Washington Times

'The whole team played **well** but I want to congratulate Walter Smith, who was tactically correct and used his team in the best way'.

Daily Record

□ 153 □

historic *and* historical

In the past, **historic** and **historical** were used interchangeably but this is no longer the case. If something is **historic** it is famous or important in history. The adjective **historical** means relating to or connected with history.

> He was making a **historic** first visit to Lebanon by a British PM – after a weekend of meetings with both Israeli and Palestinian leaders.
>
> *The Sun*

> I'm very proud to be part of this **historic** moment and I hope we never have to carry guns again.
>
> *Daily Telegraph*

> The United Nations oversaw **historic** elections in Cambodia in 1993, but Hun Sen never relinquished his grip, even though he lost.
>
> *Newsweek*

> By the mid-1940s he had published three **historical** novels set in ancient Egypt, and planned a long further series.
>
> *The Economist*

> According to most **historical** accounts, the Zulu nation was consolidated only after the departure of slaves from West Africa to the Americas.
>
> *The Guardian*

> Few British **historical** figures have been revered, revised and reviled as much as Drake.
>
> CHARLIE CONNELLY *Attention All Shipping*

hoard *and* horde

A **hoard** of something is a store or stock of it, especially a hidden none. If you **hoard** something, you store it up, often to excess, and especially in secret. A **horde** of people is a great number of them in a crowd. These two words are homophones and, as such, are often confused.

> Doors at the course open at 11am and there will be hoards of people queuing to get in.
>
> *Daily Record*

> That film was about a horde of loot hidden by the Founding Fathers behind a series of 'Da Vinci Code'-style firewalls, brain teasers and locked boxes.
>
> *Settle Times*

Try to remember that **hoard** (a store) and 'cupboard' (a place a store is kept) end in the same 4 letters.

> The items included a spectacular Viking **hoard** of 20 silver bracelets.
>
> *The Times*

> Security woes in the Middle East and Africa have made everyone jumpy and eager to **hoard** precious petroleum.
>
> *The Economist*

> Mr Spector arrived at the Los Angeles court smiling at the **hordes** of waiting journalists.
>
> *BBC Entertainment*

immoral *and* amoral

An **immoral** person or act is considered by most people to be breaking accepted moral principles or standards. An **amoral** person does not believe that there any accepted moral principles or standards. **Amoral** is also used of actions in which moral principles do not apply.

A significant majority saw Westerners as selfish, arrogant, greedy and **immoral**.

Sydney Morning Herald

Some see the displays as pornographic and **immoral**; others object to what they consider the objectification of women.

Newsweek

'We are here today because the war is illegal, **immoral** and unethical', said the Rev. Al Sharpton.

Los Angeles Times

Her best novels are generally thought to be the five describing the criminal adventures of her **amoral** psychotic anti-hero, Tom Ripley.

Chambers Biographical Dictionary

The devastating Asian tsunami inevitably gives rise to the question, is nature **amoral**, evil or good?

Newsweek

In an **amoral** world, the criminal world we lived in, he wrote a whole new chapter.

Los Angeles Times

impassable *and* impassible

If a road is **impassable**, it is not capable of being passed or travelled through. The adjective **impassible**, which means 'incapable of experiencing pain or emotion', is rarely used. People sometimes write **impassible** for **impassable**.

> Key roads snaking through the savannah turned to impassible quagmires during recent rains.
>
> *Daily Telegraph*

> There are signs that say the road may be impassible during bad weather.
>
> *Seattle Times*

Remember that **impassible** means the same as 'impassive' and both have an 'i' after the 's'.

> Kerry and Waterford are also badly affected with many roads flooded and **impassable**.
>
> *RTE News Online*

> For much of the year, the route is **impassable**: but, now that the snow has melted, the refuges are open.
>
> *Daily Telegraph*

> The weather had certainly turned bitter, with the Thames frozen over and **impassable** for boats, while the smallpox raged in London at the same time.
>
> DAPHNE DU MAURIER AND FRANCIS KING *The Winding Stair*

> The god of Judaism was a personal god with human characteristics, quite different from the remote, impersonal, and impassible deity of Greek philosophy.
>
> DELBERT ROYCE BURKETT *An Introduction to the New Testament and the Origins of Christianity*

incredible *and* incredulous

Something that is **incredible** is difficult to believe, because it is so surprising, horrifying or great. An **incredible** person or thing is exceptionally good or impressive. An **incredulous** person is someone who tends not to believe things that they are told. People sometimes use **incredulous** where **incredible** is meant.

> It is painful – almost **incredulous** – to have to repeat these words, which I first spoke at the Save Darfur rally on September 17, 2006.
>
> *Jerusalem Post*

Within the context of 'not believing', a thing is **incredible**, and a person is **incredulous**.

> I find it **incredible** that people believe we will always be subjects of the British monarch.
>
> *Sydney Morning Herald*

> Beneath the thunderous applause you could sense a collective gasp at the **incredible** performance we had just witnessed.
>
> *G&M National*

> But the United that treated an **incredulous** support to a particularly rank display at Old Trafford last night can forget all about success in the latter stages.
>
> *Glasgow Herald*

infer *and* imply

If you **infer** a meaning from something, you conclude
that it is the case from what has happened or been said
previously. If you **imply** something, you hint at it or suggest
it indirectly. Although people have been using **infer** to
mean **imply** for centuries, it is better to avoid this in formal
writing, as many people still believe it to be incorrect.

It is reasonable to **infer** that when Emma became ill with
secondary disease she would have consulted her GP in
Dorchester.

Times Literary Supplement

You have to **infer** from his actions, or lack of them, what his
real thoughts are.

The Herald

She approaches the grave, and we **infer** it is that of her late
husband.

The Guardian

Rose begins to complain as she always does, about the children
not respecting the grace she says before eating, **implying** they
have all been brought up badly.

RUSSELL CELYN JONES *Ten Seconds from the Sun*

This **implies** the housing affordability crisis is not being
caused by the cost of borrowing but the cost of housing.

Sydney Morning Herald

Strong evidence now **implies** small moons near the giant
planets like Saturn and Jupiter are essentially piles of rubble.

Science Daily

ingenious *and* ingenuous

An **ingenious** person is one who is skilled at inventing things. An **ingenious** device or plan is one that has been skilfully or cleverly contrived. An **ingenuous** person is open, honest and honourable.

> Strikingly original and **ingenious**, he designed a number of highly individualistic and unconventional buildings.
> *Chambers Biographical Dictionary*

> The tunnel screw was an **ingenious** invention that allowed the screw to drive the ship without becoming entangled by the weeds that flourish in the Nile.
> TED SIMON *Dreaming of Jupiter*

> Birmingham have launched an **ingenious** plan to woo back disgruntled supporters – by inviting them for a night out with Karren Brady and Steve Bruce.
> *Daily Mirror*

> Could there be such a thing as an **ingenuous** politician, and would we want it?
> PETER BAZALGETTE *Billion Dollar Game*

> Although he'd played **ingenuous**, he'd known right away what the man was getting at.
> NICHOLAS EVANS *The Horse Whisperer*

intense *and* intensive

Something **intense** is extreme or very great. An **intense** person is deeply emotional. If something is **intensive**, it is concentrated or unremitting. People sometimes use **intense** where **intensive** is meant.

> There are 25 species of British bumblebee but their numbers have been declining in the last 50 years due to dramatic changes in the landscape caused by intense farming.
>
> *Daily Mail*

Be careful when you use these two adjectives.

> Employers will come under **intense** pressure to make further cuts to their occupational pension schemes.
>
> *The Guardian*

> The official line is she was dehydrated after 12 hours shooting in **intense** heat.
>
> *The Sun*

> He is an **intense** and thoughtful military man who has few airs and graces, but he has a razor-sharp mind.
>
> *Sydney Morning Herald*

> Yesterday, he joined a batch of 15 recruits heading for **intensive** training at the Scottish Police College at Tulliallan in Fife.
>
> *Daily Record*

> The grey squirrel and the domestic cat are preventing the recovery of Britain's songbirds, which were devastated by **intensive farming** in the post-war years.
>
> *Daily Telegraph*

judicial *and* judicious

The adjective **judicial** signifies a connection with judges or the law. The adjective **judicious** means 'showing or possessing good judgement'.

> However, their lawyers said they would seek a **judicial** review of the convictions for their role in the 2002 Bali bombings.
> *Sydney Morning Herald*

> The university takes the charges seriously. 'We think it is important to let the Georgia **judicial** system resolve the case', the statement said.
> *The News & Observer*

> Tzivin said he understood that Israel's policy was not to interfere in the **judicial** proceedings of other countries.
> *Jerusalem Post*

> Scotland emerged as a European kingdom as a result of **judicious** marriage alliances with Norway and Flanders.
> *Chambers Biographical Dictionary*

> A national campaign has sought to promote a more **judicious** approach for prescribing antibiotics for children.
> *Science Daily*

> Through **judicious** use of the odd swearword, he strives to preserve this approach from tweeness.
> *The Guardian*

junction *and* juncture

A **junction** is a place where things, for example roads, join together. A **juncture** is a critical or important point in time.

> They found the juncture but could see no light down the other corridor, so they inched blindly forward as they had before, following the limestone walls with their fingers.
> R SCOTT BAKKER *The Warrior-Prophet*

> If the red squirrels only faced competition for food at the juvenile stage, it is unlikely they would be at such a critical junction.
> *Belfast Telegraph*

A **junction** relates to place, while a **juncture** relates to time.

> The hall is located at the **junction** at Moat Street and Union Street.
> *RTE News Online*

> Jilib is at a crucial **junction** of rivers and roads that lead to Kismayo.
> *G&M National*

> A try at that **juncture** in the game might have helped to bolster England's self-belief.
> *Daily Telegraph*

> At every critical **juncture**, many of us predicted the problems we would face and offered constructive ideas for overcoming them.
> *Time*

lay *and* lie

There is a great deal of confusion over these two verbs. If you **lay** something, you put it down. When you **lie**, you are in or get yourself into a horizontal position. Although **lay** is often used in place of **lie**, you should avoid it as many people consider it to be incorrect.

'We were **laying** in bed and he called me Lisa'.
Sydney Morning Herald

The confusion arises in part because the past tense of **lie** is **lay**. The verb **lay** is transitive, and **lie** is intransitive.

Heartbroken families of the victims **laid** flowers at the spot yesterday.

The Sun

'She wanted to run', said her husband, Afredo Anzaldo, 45, who **lays** carpet for a living.

Seattle Times

He was **lying** on a heap of cushions with Nikki and a few others who were all talking and laughing and clearly having a great time.

NICHOLAS EVANS *The Divide*

Flora neatly lays out her clothes for the morning over a chair, then undresses and **lies** in bed.

RUSSELL CELYN *Jones Ten Seconds from the Sun*

leach *and* leech

If you **leach** a substance from something solid, you remove the substance by allowing a liquid to percolate through the solid object. As a noun, a **leech** is a bloodsucking worm and, by extension, a person who gets close to another person for personal gain. The verb **leech** means 'to apply leeches to' or 'to cling like a leech to'. It also means 'to drain'.

Inorganic fertilizers also cause environmental problems associated with **leeching** into our water systems.
Science Daily

Time is a corrosive fluid, dissolving motivation, destroying novelty, and **leaching** the joy from life.
Charles Stross Glasshouse

If the meaning is 'drain or remove', the verb is **leech**. If the meaning is 'seep through', the verb is **leach**.

The cocktail of toxic substances contained in computers has the potential to **leach** into the environment at landfill sites.
Sydney Morning Herald

On the last day, we found **leeches** on our bodies.
Jerusalem Post

Sporting high heels and a range of designer dresses with revealing cleavage, Tautou plays a **leech** who preys on rich old men on the French Riviera.
Sydney Morning Herald

But I kept seeing in Home a consummate con artist – handsome, plausible and with a talent for **leeching** on his admirers.
The Herald

The leaden sky **leeched** everything of colour – except the blood.
Trudi Canavan Last of the Wilds

loath *and* loathe

Loath is an adjective meaning 'reluctant or unwilling'. It can also be spelt **loth**. **Loathe** is a verb meaning 'to dislike intensely or feel disgust at'.

> Like him or **loath** him, Fidel Castro is one of them.
> *Daily Telegraph*

> For much of the season opponents have seemed **loathe** to test him in the tackle.
> *Sydney Morning Herald*

Remember that, like 'hate' and 'dislike', the verb **loathe** ends in 'e'.

> The hit-obsessed media are **loath** to cover foreign films.
> *Newsweek*

> And he was **loath** to admit it, but May was right: he should have looked for other weapons on his captive.
> SUSANNA GREGORY *Blood on the Strand*

> He was **loth** to burden his two daughters.
> *The Economist*

> Iggy was the nickname Andrew **loathed** at Upper Canada College.
> *G&M National*

> Mr Sarkozy is admired and **loathed** in equal measure for his vocal pledges to crack down on such 'scum', as he called rioters last year.
> *Daily Telegraph*

luxurious *and* luxuriant

Something **luxurious** is characterized by luxury or indulgence. If something is **luxuriant**, it grows abundantly or profusely. The two are sometimes confused.

> Arms crossed, the lanky girl with **luxurious** hair and a lazy smile looked him over in a way that made him shiver.
> KATE ELLIOTT *Spirit Gate*

> Two red sofas, deep and **luxuriant**, sat either side of the white wooden fireplace.
> JENNY COLGAN *West End Girls*

You should use **luxuriant** when describing hair and plants, and **luxurious** in all other contexts.

> David will live between the star's **luxurious** homes in London and America.
> *Daily Mirror*

> Soften the look of wooden floors with a **luxurious** rug in a light tone.
> *The Herald*

> Her **luxuriant** hair, wound around her head, was the colour of blackest coal.
> MIKLOS VAMOS *The Book of Fathers*

> We meandered our way around The Lost Gardens of Heligan where scarlet camellias ran rampant in **luxuriant** foliage.
> *The Guardian*

meretricious *and* meritorious

Something that is **meretricious** is superficially attractive but of no real value or worth. A **meretricious** person is insincere. A **meritorious** person or thing deserves to be praised, honoured or rewarded.

> Even a lesser Scorsese movie, The Aviator in 2004, lost to the slick and **meretricious** Million Dollar Baby.
>
> *The Guardian*

> Cynical, **meretricious**, selfish, the decade made the rich richer, the poor poorer.
>
> DOMINIC SANDBROOK *Never Had It So Good*

> He thought Ménétrel to be little more than a shallow and **meretricious** scoundrel, with an undue and unwarranted influence over his aged patient.
>
> *Charles Williams Pétain*

> Funds from the dinner will be donated for scholarships to four **meritorious** students, who have passed the higher secondary exam with flying colours.
>
> *Times of India*

> The new system included military honours for **meritorious** service and bravery but nothing specifically for rare instances of military valour.
>
> *G&M National*

> What is so **meritorious** about someone going round the world really fast in an expensive boat designed to go round the world really fast?
>
> *The Herald*

mitigate *and* militate

If you **mitigate** something bad, you make it less severe or more bearable. If an action or fact **militates** for or against something, it has an effect or influence on that thing. People often use **mitigate for** or **against** when it should be **militate**.

'Hopefully, this will help mitigate against job losses'.

The Herald

The verb **mitigate** takes a direct object, while **militate** is followed by a preposition such as 'against' or 'for'.

Not only that, the drug appeared to **mitigate** the effects of chemotherapy.

Newsweek

Major Couture said the coalition is doing all that it can to **mitigate** the risks to its soldiers involved in resupply missions.

G&M National

We believe that the international community is right to place pressure on Hamas to change those policies which **militate** against a peace process.

Jerusalem Post

In other words, all sorts of things were **militating** toward a certain amount of exhaustion with Bush.

National Review Online

obsolete *and* obsolescent

Something that is **obsolete** is outdated and no longer in use. Something **obsolescent** is going out of date and is still in the process of disappearing and becoming useless.

Although the Pony Express was almost immediately made **obsolete** by the telegraph, it lives on in US legend as an emblem of American inventiveness and daring.
Chambers Dictionary of World History

After one of its missiles destroyed an **obsolete** weather satellite on Jan 11, Beijing said the strike was a test for 'scientific' purposes.
Daily Telegraph

It was the hulls of **obsolete** naval vessels, both British and captured foreign ships, that were used as prison hulks.
Roy Adkins and Lesley Adkins *The War for All the Oceans*

Coil Steels Group has joined a growing list of industrial users relocating from **obsolescent** industrial accommodation to new, purpose-built warehousing.
Sydney Morning Herald

If, therefore, the government acts quickly, it is still possible to avoid 'loss of power' blackouts when the UK's **obsolescent** power stations are closed in the 2020s.
The Herald

□ 170 □

official *and* officious

Something that is **official** relates to, or is authorized or issued by a public authority or office. Someone **officious** is too forward in offering unwanted or unwelcome services.

The final text will now be translated into all the **official** languages of the EU and formally adopted in the near future.
Computing UK

The band released a number of tickets via their **official** website yesterday for members of the group's official mailing list.
New Musical Express

Last week an **official** inquiry strongly criticized the Canadian police for incompetence and dishonesty.
RTE News Online

He began gaining more worldwide recognition with his role as an **officious** bureaucrat in the Terry Gilliam's movie Brazil in1985.
Daily Record

'No doubt wardens can be **officious,** over-zealous and often wrong: 56 per cent of challenges to tickets in London were upheld last year. But they are also fall guys for the system'.
Sydney Morning Herald

paramount *and* tantamount

If something is **paramount**, it is supreme or superior to all others. If something is **tantamount to** something else, the two are equal in value or meaning.

Two aspects are **paramount** – public order and road safety.
Belfast Telegraph

The welfare of players is **paramount** to our continued existence as an entity, and it is a national duty for us.
Rugby World

The education of the children is of **paramount** importance and it is disappointing that the school was unable to reach a compromise in this case.
Daily Mirror

Health officials were warning that distributing clean injecting equipment was **tantamount** to condoning drug use.
Sydney Morning Herald

Pyongyang said that new U.N. sanctions are **tantamount** to a declaration of war.
Washington Times

'Well, a loveless marriage is **tantamount** to hell', said Audrey to herself.
Marilyn Heward Mills Cloth Girl

partly *and* partially

These two adverbs should not be treated as synonyms. **Partly** means 'in part' or 'in some degree'. **Partially** means 'not totally or entirely'.

She knew she was **partly** to blame for their all being so lazy around the house.

Jane Blanchard Fanning Old Flames

People take risks **partly** because they believe that unpleasant events, like car crashes, only happen to other people.

Sydney Morning Herald

The study was **partly** funded through grants from the American Parkinson Disease Association and American Health Assistance Foundation.

Science Daily

En masse the administration departed for Pyinmana, a **partially** completed new city 320 kilometres north, with virtually no communications links to the outside world.

Sydney Morning Herald

Witnesses said Israeli forces **partially** destroyed the Dar al-Hikma hospital in Baalbek.

Seattle Times

He is **partially** deaf in his right ear after an accident.

Daily Record

pathos *and* bathos

Pathos is the quality that arouses pity. Its related adjective is **pathetic**, the original meaning of which is 'arousing pity or sorrow'. **Bathos** is a ludicrous descent from elevated subject matter or style to the ordinary, either in speech or writing. Its related adjective is **bathetic**.

The **pathos** of the child who can never come home is one of the most compelling ways in which ghost stories connect writers and readers with loss.

Times Literary Supplement

There was grittiness and **pathos** in her pursuit of celebrity; she was an underdog some cheered for.

Newsweek

He now cuts a **pathetic** figure, his face badly deformed by repeated gangland beatings, stabbings and stampings.

Daily Record

The fate of John Major's government should serve as a warning. Without any clear idea of what they were doing, ministers succumbed to the **bathos** of the highway 'cones hotline'.

The Economist

It was a curiously **bathetic** contrast to the climactic suspense of an afternoon in which fingernails must have been bitten to the bone across France and Ireland.

The Guardian

peremptory *and* perfunctory

A **peremptory** instruction or comment is one that is arrogantly made and cannot be denied or ignored. A **perfunctory** action is done without enthusiasm or interest, merely as a duty to be got through, and in a hasty or superficial way. People sometimes use **peremptory** when **perfunctory** is meant.

> After a peremptory trial he was shot dead on 21 March and buried in a shallow grave in the dry moat.
> ROY ADKINS AND LESLEY ADKINS *The War for All the Oceans*

> Criminals, selected precisely because they were the most serious in their age group, were subject to only the most peremptory supervision.
> *Daily Telegraph*

Perfunctory is more commonly used than **peremptory**, so take time to check it is **peremptory** you mean to use.

> Nor did Friedan's famously brusque and **peremptory** manner make her an easy ally.
> *Sydney Morning Herald*

> William gave a **peremptory** signal to the knights of his mesnie.
> ELIZABETH CHADWICK *The Scarlet Lion*

> He could not understand why the boy was asking since he rarely exchanged more than the most **perfunctory** few words with his mother-in-law.
> *Jerusalem Post*

> When it was time to go, her response to Robert's farewell kiss was little more than **perfunctory**.
> NICHOLAS EVANS *The Horse Whisperer*

perverse *and* perverted

Someone who is **perverse** deliberately behaves in a manner considered to be wrong or abnormal, often in order to irritate other people. Their behaviour can also be described as **perverse**. Someone who is **perverted** has sexual desires that most people consider to be abnormal or highly improper. Therefore their behaviour is **perverted**.

It was typical of his father, Thorne thought, to be so **perverse**, so bloody-minded.

MARK BILLINGHAM *Buried*

She seems to take a **perverse** delight in the fact that most of the songs are her least popular.

G&M National

Hatcher risked her career as a Hollywood star to put her **perverted** uncle behind bars 30 years after he repeatedly molested her as a child.

New York Post

He sent her letters fantasising about **perverted** sex with knives and bondage.

The Sun

pitiable, pitiful *and* piteous

These three adjectives share some meanings, but cannot always be used interchangeably. **Pitiable, pitiful** and **piteous** all mean 'arousing or deserving pity'. **Pitiable** and **pitiful** can also mean 'contemptible or miserable'. You cannot use **piteous** in that sense.

> But the most **pitiable** victims of cholera were the native labourers. One headman lost 146 of the 160 workers he brought from Malaya to the railway within two months.
>
> BRIAN MACARTHUR *Surviving the Sword*

> Chingoka has become a **pitiful** figure. To look at him nowadays is to see a man who knows the corruption of his soul.
>
> *Sydney Morning Herald*

> We were told that Miss Fitzgerald continued periodically to visit the shrine of her lamented brother, and that her piercing and **piteous** cries made it a most afflicting scene to witness.
>
> ROY ADKINS AND LESLEY ADKINS *The War for All the Oceans*

> He had the misfortune to get all that attention, and to put on his **pitiable** display before Congress, and so he is the handiest target for retribution.
>
> *Philadelphia Online*

> Villa's defence twice made **pitiful** attempts at clearances before Ji-Sung Park opened the scoring.
>
> *Daily Telegraph*

populace *and* populous

These words are homophones and therefore sometimes confused. The **populace** are the people living in a place, especially those not distinguished by rank or education. If a place is **populous** it is full of people.

> It's superficial stuff, fine for the general **populous**, but where are these people who are going to be the drivers and leaders of tomorrow?
>
> *The Guardian*

> The fact is that in a UK context, Scotland, particularly the **populace** part of it, is too often seen as a rundown place.
>
> *The Herald*

The two can be easily distinguished by their endings. **Populace** has the '–ace' ending that is common in nouns, and **populous** has the '–ous' ending that is common in adjectives.

> The senator still needs to showcase her womanly side to the general **populace.**
>
> *Philadelphia Online*

> Yet as the latter's star continues to wane among the French **populace**, a new figure has burst upon the scene.
>
> *Newsweek International*

> The election is tremendously important for Africa's most **populous** nation.
>
> *The Economist*

> Demand for broadband access is strongest in the most **populous areas** such as London, which offer providers the highest potential return.
>
> *Computing UK*

practical *and* practicable

Something **practical** is concerned with real practice, conditions or results, as opposed to theoretical ones. Something **practical** is something that is efficient. A **practical** person is concerned with real practice rather than theory. Something **practicable** is capable of being accomplished, carried out or used.

Howard Stapleton's research into noise has more **practical** applications.

G&M National

Data retention practices depend largely on the diverse nature of our data as well as the **practical** considerations of storage costs and processing system requirements.

Los Angeles Times

We need a new direction to deal in a **practical** way with the climate change challenge.

Sydney Morning Herald

Such logical, **practical**, down-to-earth people as the Romans must have been baffled by a race whose outlook on life was so radically dissimilar to their own.

Sins of the Fathers

Thomas Hare's proposal for electoral reform was not a very **practicable** one, but others soon converted its essential principles into the single transferable vote.

The Times

Air freight was now the only **practicable** method, and I had researched it thoroughly.

TED SIMON *Dreaming of Jupiter*

prescribe *and* proscribe

If you **prescribe** a course of action, you give orders for that course of action to be carried out. If you **proscribe** an activity, you prohibit it or make it illegal.

Teachers complain of being unable to tailor lessons to the backgrounds and interests of pupils because so much of what they teach is **prescribed** by the Government.

Daily Telegraph

It is alleged major offenders include traders who produce halal meat by slaughtering animals in the way **prescribed** by Islamic sharia law.

The Herald

Study Group members aren't just **prescribing** a new Iraq strategy, they're calling for a change in the way the Bush administration does business both home and abroad.

The Slate

Kembo Mohadi, the home affairs minister, verbally informed an opposition politician that the cabinet had decided to **proscribe** all rallies last week.

Daily Telegraph

Admittedly, with Belichick **proscribing** his assistants from talking to the press, it's sometimes hard to be sure.

Newsweek

The state could promote its interest in the 'potentiality of human life' by regulation, even to the point of **proscribing** abortion outright.

National Review Online

The related nouns are **prescription** and **proscription**.

presume *and* assume

If you **presume** something to be the case, you suppose
that it is so, even though you have no proof. If you **assume**
something to be the case, you take it for granted that it is so.
Assume implies a stronger level of belief in something than
presume; **presume** acknowledges a lack of proof.

> I watch a while longer and I can see her lips moving in what I
> **presume** must be a prayer.
>
> *Daily Telegraph*

> As I spoke, I noticed a neatly dressed man whom I **presumed**
> was American listening to us carefully, moving closer.
>
> *The Guardian*

> When we saw Mr Reeves pull up in a white van we **presumed**
> there was furniture in it and offered our help.
>
> *The Sun*

> He is wearily resigned to the fact that people **assume** he
> cannot sing just because he used to play sport for a living.
>
> *Sydney Morning Herald*

> 'I **assume** you would like to be revenged on the murderers of
> your wife'.
>
> KJ PARKER *Evil for Evil*

> The landlord said it had been parked there on Tuesday evening.
> He had not reported it initially because he **assumed** that one
> of his customers had left it there overnight.
>
> *Daily Telegraph*

prevaricate *and* procrastinate

If you **prevaricate**, you avoid stating the truth or coming directly to the point. If you **procrastinate**, you put off doing something that should be done immediately. People sometimes confuse these two verbs.

> My plan had worked perfectly until now, but I still lacked the confidence to use my own words to ask for what I wanted. And so I prevaricated, never even setting pen to paper.
> *Michelle Lovric The Remedy*

These verbs are not synonymous.

> 'I'll see how things go, Joe', she **prevaricated**. 'Let's just leave it at that'.
> EMMA BLAIR *Sweethearts*

> Rather than give a straight 'No', I **prevaricated**, saying I was too busy because of the bomb squad's visit.
> JOHN TULLOCH *One Day in July*

> Everyone **procrastinates** on their homework to some extent.
> *Seattle Times*

> That may have prompted shoppers to **procrastinate** a little longer than in previous years. 'With Christmas on Monday, I had the whole weekend to think about shopping', said Chris Bowie.
> *Washington Times*

principle *and* principal

A **principle** is a rule, law or fundamental truth. A **principal** is a person of the highest rank, for example in a university or school. A **principal** person or thing is highest in rank or importance.

He said most wave-energy designs operate on **principals** of buoyancy.

Engineer Technology

His three jockeys all agree Desert Orchid's **principle** qualities were his immense intelligence, his bravery and his durability.

Daily Telegraph

Principle and **principal** are often confused.

Good to see that **principles** are alive and well in our political leadership.

Sydney Morning Herald

A democracy founded on the **principles** of freedom and tolerance does not kill religious dissenters.

Washington Times

Bill, his father, was a high-school **principal.**

Seattle Times

Thomas Lund, **principal** dancer at the Royal Danish Ballet, won best male dancer at the ceremony on Thursday.

BBC Entertainment

prostrate *and* prostate

A person who is **prostrate** is lying with their face on the ground. If you **prostrate** yourself, you throw yourself forwards onto the ground. The **prostate** is a gland that males have at the neck of the bladder.

> The research team had previously demonstrated that injection of Botox into the **prostrate** gland produced improvement in symptoms.
>
> *Science Daily*

Remember that the word that refers to the body part is **prostate**, without the 'r'.

> With some difficulty she crawled from beneath the bed and lay **prostrate** at Margaret's feet.
>
> SANDI TOKSVIG *Melted Into Air*

> He pointed to where the ambassador had **prostrated** himself on the ground after he had delivered his ruler's letters.
>
> SUSANNA GREGORY *A Conspiracy of Violence*

> A conference on **prostate** cancer was opened today in Dublin by the society's chief executive, John McCormack.
>
> *RTE News Online*

purposefully *and* purposely

These two adverbs are often confused. If you do something **purposefully**, you do it in a manner that has a definite purpose in mind. If you do something **purposely**, you intended to do it and it did not happen by accident.

Someone has done this purposefully and knew we had gone out.

Times of India

Keen to draw attention to her new look, she strode purposely down the street of one of London's most fashionable areas in a daring mini-skirt.

Daily Mail

The adverb **purposely** is used more often in American and Canadian English than in British English, where 'on purpose' is preferred.

He was seething as he strode **purposefully** towards Merk and started mouthing off and pointing his finger at him before the referee was joined by his linesmen.

Sydney Morning Herald

Thorne turned to see two young men moving **purposefully** across the room.

MARK BILLINGHAM *The Burning Girl*

'I think they're **purposely** withholding additional information'.

Washington Times

Someone **purposely** gave him wrong directions, then robbed and killed him, the reports said.

G&M National

refute, repudiate *and* deny

These verbs relate to the same idea of 'defending oneself against an accusation', but they are not synonyms. If you **refute** an accusation, you prove that it is not the case. If you **repudiate** an accusation, you deny it, saying that it is unfounded. If you **deny** an accusation, you say that it is not true.

It was intended to **refute** a prevailing post-war myth: higher education kept women from adapting to their roles as wives and mothers.

Sydney Morning Herald

Nevertheless, this exhibition may revive such controversy, so I'd welcome the opportunity to **refute** such suggestions once and for all.

SALLY BEAUMAN *The Landscape of Love*

Brown also **repudiated** suggestions that he had been an '11th-hour' supporter of the war to topple Saddam Hussein.

Jerusalem Post

She wrote to the Protector, demanding that the Privy Council repudiate the rumour that she was in the Tower and pregnant by the Lord Admiral.

MARY S LOVELL *Bess of Hardwick*

Both Rahul and Shweta have vehemently **denied** that their marriage was on the rocks.

Times of India

Aniston's spokesman **denied** she had plastic surgery.

Daily Mirror

seasonal *and* seasonable

If something is **seasonal**, it changes or happens according to the seasons of the year. Food that is **seasonal** is available only in certain seasons. If something is **seasonable**, it is appropriate to the particular season.

> Certain kinds of animals, particularly shore birds and waterfowl, are extremely sensitive to water levels – both the amount of water available and the timing of **seasonal** rainfalls.
>
> *Science Daily*

> The most popular destinations for **seasonal** workers are Italy and Spain.
>
> *Daily Telegraph*

> Kebabs, a big draw here, are accompanied by **seasonal** vegetables, rice and grilled tomatoes.
>
> *San Francisco Chronicle*

> He was no farmer, but he knew what farmers needed: rain, sun, and **seasonable** weather.
>
> KATE ELLIOTT *In The Ruins*

The related adverbs are **seasonally** and **seasonably**.

> Occurring **seasonally** on males, the antlers sweep from front to back in one continuous curve.
>
> *Science Daily*

> I had a fruit salad that was a salad made from fruit – most of which was **seasonably** exotic.
>
> *The Times*

sensual *and* sensuous

Sensual means 'of the senses, as distinct from the mind'.
Something **sensual** provides physical gratification,
especially sexual gratification. Something that is **sensuous**
is pleasing to the senses. When the pleasure is physical, the
adjective used is **sensual**. If something pleases the senses of
sight or hearing, the adjective used is usually **sensuous**.

> During Ramadan, Muslims abstain from food, drink and
> **sensual** pleasures from sunrise to sunset in order to focus on
> their relationship with God.
>
> *Seattle Times*

> Yet again, all they'd done was kiss. A very deep, **sensual** kiss in
> the back of a taxi – but still, no more than a kiss.
>
> DEBORAH WRIGHT *Love Eternally*

> His fiction, dense with symbolism and **sensuous** imagery, has
> little in the way of conventional plot or character. *The Guardian*

> The fig is considered to be one of the most **sensual** of fruits
> with its tempting, luscious flesh that is at its best when it has
> been left to ripen in the sunshine.
>
> *BBC Food Magazine*

> He switches on the gramophone, and the hit song of the day, a
> **sensuous** waltz, floats upon the air.
>
> DAPHNE DU MAURIER *The Rebecca Notebook
> and Other Memories*

specially *and* especially

Something done **specially** is done for a particular purpose
or person. **Especially** means 'above all'. They are often
confused.

> These people know their ferns, and you'll find a fine selection
> of deciduous and evergreen ferns for sale, especially selected
> for the Northwest.
>
> *Seattle Times*

If you are in doubt, it is safer to use **specially** than
especially.

> Stephen Kappes is said to have flown in **specially** for the
> meeting between US Vice President Dick Cheney and the
> Pakistani leader on Monday.
>
> *Times of India*

> And he queried why the **specially** trained sniffer dogs did not
> react to the front seat of the burnt-out car where Mrs Harron
> was allegedly sitting and bleeding.
>
> *Belfast Telegraph*

> But I was definitely picked on, **especially** by other girls.
>
> *Daily Record*

> Yes, some people do have persistently uncomfortable feelings
> in their legs, **especially** at night.
>
> *Financial Times*

squash *and* quash

If you **squash** something, you press it down flat or squeeze it into a pulp. If a demonstration, rebellion or rumour is **quashed**, it is suppressed forcefully and suddenly. If a conviction is **quashed**, it is overturned in court.

> Most of the additional 20,000-plus American soldiers are now in Baghdad as a campaign gets underway to **squash** sectarian fighting in the capital.
>
> *The Economist*

For literal sense of 'crushing' you should use **squash**; use **quash** when it is the figurative sense.

> She **squashed** her cigarette under her shoe, stuck out her tongue at the most insolent of the schoolgirls, and strode off.
>
> *Nicholas Evans The Divide*

> He killed dozens of sheep and rabbits, stole honey, strolled nonchalantly through mountain villages and **squashed** a guinea-pig.
>
> *The Times*

> However, after the late King Hassan II **quashed** a rebellion in 1958 when still crown prince, the Rif fell into disfavour.
>
> *The Economist*

> Pop Idol Michelle McManus has **quashed** rumours she is about to become a mum.
>
> *Daily Record*

> But his convictions were **quashed** on appeal this month, and his five-year jail sentence overturned.
>
> *Sydney Morning Herald*

stationary *and* stationery

Something or someone that is **stationary** is not moving. **Stationery** is paper and writing materials such as pens and pencils. As homophones, the two are sometimes confused.

> Perhaps the most bizarre sight was the lions slumped under the body of stationery jeeps, resting innocuously in the shade: it was hard to believe they're killers of the first degree.
>
> *The Guardian*

> To most people, a name-change wouldn't mean much. None of the buildings being built on Lichtin Boulevard are finished, so nobody will have to change stationary letterhead.
>
> *The News & Observer*

One way to distinguish between the two is to remember that **stationery** has an 'e', as in 'envelope'.

> He sped off, hitting a **stationary** car before running away.
>
> *Daily Mirror*

> Television pictures showed a mass of emergency vehicles and **stationary** traffic outside the embassy as the area was sealed off.
>
> *BBC News*

> The expenses also cover such things as overnight accommodation in London, travel, buying computers and **stationery**.
>
> *The Herald*

> Last November, for example, Metcalfe provoked derision by ordering **stationery**, coffee mugs and computer screensavers for staff, emblazoned with the department's new slogan.
>
> *Sydney Morning Herald*

sympathy *and* empathy

Many people struggle to understand the difference between these two abstract nouns. If you have **sympathy** for another person, you feel pity or compassion for them. If you have **empathy** for or with another person, you are able to imagine yourself in their place, experiencing the things they experience.

> He knows a tidal **wave of sympathy** is heading his way from his adoring Irish public in the wake of his wife Heather's death from breast cancer last month.
>
> *Daily Record*

> It strikes me as petty and ungrateful, and I have no **sympathy** for parents who are unhappy that they didn't have a son or a daughter.
>
> *Newsweek*

> Maybe it was the pizza boxes that did it, that gave me a sudden pang of understanding and **empathy for** Linda. My own kitchen looked the same, a lot of the time, minus the microwave.
>
> JIM BUTCHER *Storm Front*

> Crucially, we wanted the audience to feel **empathy** with the performers, to feel that they, too, were small and locked into an outsized, inhospitable space with larger, often menacing figures lurking outside.
>
> *The Guardian*

The related adjectives are **sympathetic** and **empathetic** and the related verbs are **sympathize** and **empathize**.

titillate *and* titivate

Something that **titillates** a person tickles or stimulates them, especially in a sexual way. If you **titivate** a place or an object, you smarten it up.

> Alleged death threats, phone bugging operations and under-the-table payments to underworld figure Mick Gatto to smooth relations with building unions were among the more **titillating** revelations.
>
> *Sydney Morning Herald*

> Clark's work gets right at the bizarre piety of a modern popular culture that's saturated with **titillating** images of Lindsay, Britney, and Mary-Kate and Ashley, but that also reacts with vituperation when any artist attempts to dig beneath those images.
>
> *The Slate*

> To the Pyes it seemed that in the years they had been living out of the country, **titivating** their houses had become a major English pastime, a compulsive new game.
>
> NINA BAWDEN *Family Money*

> At the table I thought, again, how ghastly the room was. Gordon has **titivated** it. There are new lampshades, different paintings. But it's still low-ceilinged, claustrophobic and gloomy.
>
> *The Times*

tortuous *and* torturous

A **tortuous** road is full of twists and bends. A **tortuous** process or plan takes a long time to come into being and is far from straightforward. Something that is **torturous** involves or resembles torture.

> As the driver snakes along **tortuous** roads, Mortenson knows that any miscalculation could send the vehicle tumbling over cliffs.
>
> *The Christian Science Monitor*

> The five-year development of Vista has been one of the most **tortuous** processes in Microsoft's history.
>
> *The Guardian*

> If this **tortuous** plan succeeded, an election would be called. If it failed, the Assembly would be scrapped.
>
> *Belfast Telegraph*

> That was worse than the **torturous** back pain caused by his crumbling bones.
>
> *Seattle Times*

> In the recent Tour de Suisse, which had more than 220 kilometres of **torturous** climbing, Evans had a bit of trouble with the pollen.
>
> *Sydney Morning Herald*

> The whole event was depressingly predictable. It looks as if it has been a **torturous** experience for the players – it's certainly been **torturous** for the spectators.
>
> *Daily Telegraph*

unwanted *and* unwonted

If a person or thing is **unwanted**, it is not wanted or desired.
If something is **unwonted**, it is unusual.

> Anything that brings down the rate of **unwanted** pregnancies
> should be looked at very seriously.
>
> *The Herald*

> Some have deployed thugs to keep **unwanted** visitors at bay.
>
> *The Economist*

> UK companies spend an estimated £1.3bn per year on filtering
> and dealing with **unwanted** mail.
>
> *Computing UK*

> It was something of a shock last week when Dead-Eye Dick
> Cheney took his marksman's skills into the Russian arena and
> took aim – with **unwonted** accuracy – at the true nature of Mr
> Putin's regime.
>
> *The Times*

> There remains only the matter of aching limbs, stretched into
> **unwonted** positions that correspond to an elephant's girth.
>
> *Daily Telegraph*

> 'I'd want to see my kids and Sheila provided for, check up on
> her pension rights, make sure the insurance was up to date and
> so on', Kite said with **unwonted** sobriety.
>
> MARJORIE ECCLES *The Gil Mayo Mysteries Omnibus*

venal *and* venial

A **venal** person or organization is open to bribery or able to be corrupted by money. If a mistake is **venial**, it is easily excused or pardoned. It is found most often in **venial sin**, a term in Christianity referring to a sin that does not result in spiritual death. People sometimes write **venal sin** instead of **venial sin**.

> But when it does, there will remain a scandal of gambling, match-fixing and other venal sins for the country to confront.
>
> *Newsweek*

The correct phrase is **venial sin**: both words contain the letter 'i'.

> He accepted that corruption was endemic, that the government was **venal** and incompetent, and that much of the international aid was wasted, or 'inefficiently used'.
>
> MICHAEL HOLMAN *Last Orders at Harrods*

> But Cervantes did not enjoy the fruits of his labours, having signed away his copyright to a **venal** publisher.
>
> *The Herald*

> 'So if I stole two and fivepence, it would only be a **venial sin**?'
> 'Ye-es', said Nanda, a little doubtfully.
>
> ANTONIA WHITE *Frost in May*

> Julie had brought the kitten into the chapel with her for the daily cleaning, not an invitation of which Imelda would approve but a **venial sin** rather than a mortal one.
>
> FRANCES FYFIELD *Sarah Fortune Collection*

veracity *and* voracity

Veracity is truthfulness. It is derived from Latin *vērus*, meaning 'true'. **Voracity** is greed. It is derived from Latin *vorāre*, meaning 'to devour'.

> Meanwhile, Costello seemed to confirm his own reputation as a whining hypocrite, despite the apparent **veracity** of his recollections.
>
> *London Review of Books*

> 'Gonzalez has claimed that he was acting under the control of voices, that he was being compelled by the voices to kill. We do not accept the **veracity** of those claims'.
>
> *The Times*

> Questions were also asked about the **veracity** of her story of her life before the accident.
>
> *Daily Telegraph*

> The man took the sandwiches without thanks, opened and ate them with the **voracity** of a dog before the daily bowl, swallowing rather than chewing.
>
> FRANCES FYFIELD *Sarah Fortune Collection*

> Wedged between these desperate dramas of alcoholism, addiction, incest, madness, sexual **voracity** and violence, Period of Adjustment – a situation comedy about middle-class marriage – came as a pleasant surprise to audiences and critics alike.
>
> *The Guardian*

> And for those who don't have that **voracity** for cocoa ... well, it's just a matter of time.
>
> *San Francisco Chronicle*

vocation *and* avocation

A **vocation** is an occupation or profession, especially one that demands skill and dedication. An **avocation** is a diversion or distraction from your regular employment. It comes from Latin *ab*, meaning 'from' and *vocāre*, meaning 'to call'. Sometimes **avocation** is used where **vocation** is meant. You should avoid this usage as it is not standard.

> He spent five years in Catholic boarding schools, and aspired to be a priest. He spent four years in a seminary but decided the **vocation** was not for him.
>
> *Sydney Morning Herald*

> But my **true vocation**, the thing that binds me to life, is writing novels.
>
> *The Guardian*

> And of course there was his activism – a common **avocation** in the ferment of the 1960s, perhaps, but hardly typical of the bookish rabbis and academics who were his colleagues.
>
> *Jerusalem Post*

> Baseball filled my life, growing from **avocation** to obsession as I grew from six to eleven.
>
> *Newsweek*

wet *and* whet

These two verbs are sometimes confused. If you **wet** something, you make it damp. If you **whet** an object, you sharpen it by rubbing. If you **whet** an interest or an appetite, you make it keen or excite it.

> Eagerly-anticipated thriller Sunshine hits our screens on Thursday. But if you can't wait till then, I've got an exclusive clip from the movie to **wet** your appetite.
>
> *The Sun*

In many accents, although not all, they are homophones. This contributes to the occasional confusion.

> Rain continued to pour inward, **wetting** his hands and making it impossible to get the grip he needed.
>
> NICHOLAS SPARKS *Message in a Bottle*

> His heart-rate seemed to have doubled. He took a sip of lukewarm coffee **to wet** his dry mouth.
>
> JEREMY DYSON *Never Trust a Rabbit*

> 'This learning game is all very well', Norton went on, **whetting** an inappropriately large knife on a stone he had removed from the pouch at his side.
>
> SUSANNA GREGORY *The Mark of a Murderer*

> The fresh air had **whetted** his appetite and there was time, before his meeting, to eat in one of the town's inns.
>
> ALEX THOMSON AND NIC COMPTON *Voices from the Sea*

> Having spent 48 hours in St Andrews earlier this week, my appetite is already **whetted** for this year's Open Championship.
>
> *The Herald*

wrapped *and* rapt

Something that is **wrapped** is enclosed in a material such as paper or fabric. If you are **wrapped up** in something, you are completely engrossed in it or absorbed in it. If you describe a person as **rapt**, they are so absorbed in something it is as if they have been entranced by it.

> Christmas was on the horizon and, for the first and last time, I already had in advance a number of **wrapped** presents.
> WILL RANDALL *Another Long Day on the Piste*

> The passengers were still **wrapped up** in conversation, not yet having noticed anything unusual.
> CHARLES STROSS *Iron Sunrise*

> After that it was total silence as they sat mesmerised taking in every word with **rapt** attention.
> *Times of India*

> From her vantage point, Sullivan saw exactly what Obama saw – 1,500 **rapt** faces staring up at him with curiosity, affection and hope.
> *Salon Magazine*

When you are describing a state of total concentration or attention, you should use **rapt** (not wrapped) or **wrapped up** (not rapt up).